# DRAWING D-DAY

# DRAWING
# D-DAY

## An Artist's Journey Through War

### UGO GIANNINI

#### WITH
#### MAXINE GIANNINI

DOVER PUBLICATIONS, INC.
MINEOLA, NEW YORK

*Bibliographical Note*

This Dover edition, first published in 2019, is an unabridged republication of the work originally published by AuthorHouse, Bloomington, Indiana, in 2013. This edition adds "The Place of Giant Trees," a new poem by Laura Giannini.

*International Standard Book Number*

*ISBN-13: 978-0-486-83242-5*
*ISBN-10: 0-486-83242-2*

Manufactured in China by RR Donnelley
83242201    2019
www.doverpublications.com

*"One step beyond that line, reminiscent*

*of the line separating the living from the dead,*

*and it's the unknown suffering and death."*

*—Leo Tolstoy, WAR AND PEACE*

# CONTENTS

# THE PLACE OF GIANT TREES

By Laura Giannini

I remember going there
and finding in that hidden wood
a place of giant trees—
That was in France/a secret garden
of growing giants—
Trees whose width and mass and weight
blocked out the sun's rays
those ten-ton giants
and you were also one—
My father—the day you died
the men came and felled
in front of our house
an ancient tree/with an enormous thud
like a heart being ripped
from a chest/it crashed
the length of our street.
At that same moment
you too fell from this life.
Never has a tree seemed
more human and you
more like a tree
  at that moment
of your death/and the tree's death
the men sawing its trunk
into dozens of logs

I felt its bleeding
as I felt your own blood
now mixing with the sawdust
you both have
    become.

And yet the tree's spirit
mixing with your own
and becoming/the wind—
    one breath howling
    through the open branches
    through the doors of our house—
You became a giant oak
my father—your ancient stories remembered
ring by ring.

The trees for the telling
to write on
the tree's pith and center
ghost branches
a sky print
shadows surround you
ancient one now lying in dirt
sprouting a tree/a giant oak
    from your head.

# FOREWORD

By Joseph Balkoski, author of
*Beyond the Beachhead: The 29th Infantry
Division in Normandy*

Over the past three decades, I have had the privilege of knowing hundreds of veterans of the U.S. Army's 29th Infantry Division, a unit that during World War II landed on Omaha Beach on D-Day and fought nearly continuously for eleven months, suffering more than 20,000 casualties, until Nazi Germany was toppled and the war in Europe was won. The overriding lesson of my relationship with those veterans is that men who have experienced war at its worst bear in their psyches a barrier, nearly impenetrable to all except their wartime comrades. It is in truth a defense mechanism, a means that allowed thousands of emotionally scarred men to proceed with the rest of their lives with as much normality as possible: finding jobs, raising families, and doing all the things returning GIs were expected to do. But in an era when the phrase "post-traumatic stress disorder" did not exist, men who had indeed suffered severe trauma had to carry on a ceaseless struggle, for the most part internalized, to pursue their goals in a world filled with civilians who could not comprehend their innermost thoughts.

They called themselves "Twenty-Niners," and one of them I came to know over the years, regrettably only in spirit rather than in the flesh, was a remarkable man named Ugo Giannini. What immediately struck me about Ugo was that he was about as different from the typical 29th Division "dogface soldier" as it was possible to be. Upon entry into the Army he joined a 29th Division infantry regiment filled with southern boys, and it must have been curious for him, the child of Italian immigrants from East Orange, New Jersey, to be thrown into the closed world of a highly motivated military unit comprised of young men with entirely different backgrounds than his own. But from those men Ugo learned how to be a good soldier. Had it not been for his transfer to the 29th Division military police unit shortly before D-Day, he would have accompanied those men into battle, fighting a ruthless and nearly daily struggle against a resolute enemy, starting with the Normandy invasion on June 6, 1944. As he noted in a letter to his girl back home after V-E Day, had he fought that kind of war, "I assure you I would have been dead by now."

From the ranks of U.S. Army riflemen in World War II, one does not expect to find many budding Hemingways, or Twains, or Fitzgeralds. But from the first moment I perused Ugo Giannini's wartime correspondence, for the most part written in or close to the front lines in the midst of combat, I was astonished to discover that he possessed an extraordinarily rare talent for written communication, one that effectively evoked the sights and sounds of war as they actually were experienced by the men who fought it. So powerful was his prose that he simultaneously mesmerized and unnerved the amazed recipients of his letters. To read Ugo's wartime writing is to have a momentary window inside the psyche of an exceptional soldier, a window he would soon seal up forever. "I still can't quite grasp it," he wrote at the war's end. "How did I come through it without a scratch?"

Ugo also possessed a remarkable talent for drawing, an aptitude that he first demonstrated as a child and was refined in the prewar years at the National Academy of Design in New York. When he joined the army, he continued to practice that skill, producing drawings of frontline soldiers that emerged from his own personal visions of combat, most notably of the cataclysm of the 29th Division's landing on Omaha Beach on D-Day. His artwork so impressed the 29th Division's top brass that his services were regularly called for to illustrate the covers of the 29th's after-action reports throughout the war.

When Ugo finally returned stateside after V-E Day, and his ability to speak of the war in written or spoken words gradually diminished and eventually faded to almost nothing, he found an emotional outlet in his art and ultimately was consumed by it. What surfaced in one brilliant painting after another was in effect a silent salute to the men of the 29th Division, Ugo's wartime comrades, whose sacrifice by the thousands he could not let go. Viewers of those paintings can begin to understand not only the trauma of war, but also its personal impact upon the artist.

The publication of Ugo Giannini's unique wartime and postwar artwork, alongside his evocative words on his career in the renowned 29th Division, is long overdue. His art and prose now belong to the ages.

# PREFACE

By Maxine Giannini

The fortieth anniversary of the D-Day landings was June 6, 1984. "Red" Holland and Verne Johnson, who had been Ugo's commanding officers, had contacted him beforehand, wanting to reunite and return to the beach for the ceremonies. There seemed to be a special affection for Ugo in the MP Platoon. Upon hearing of his death in 1993, Rex Potts, his sergeant, said, "How I loved that man."

The last time Ugo had been on the beach was in 1948, four years after the invasion. He and Arnold Herstand returned to Paris under the GI Bill (this was a stipend given to ex-GIs by the government to complete their schooling; it educated a generation who would have not had the opportunity) and persuaded painter Fernand Léger to open an atelier for the GIs, where Ugo studied. Ugo was still wearing his GI boots and khaki trousers. He met a man named Tom Van Dyke, who was a documentary filmmaker. They returned to Omaha Beach and made a film about the invasion. Although it was made for the fifth anniversary, the film was never released. No one knows where it is today.

In 1984, Ugo could not return, whatever the reasons—emotional, physical, psychological. But it was then that his longest journey back to Omaha and the events of WWII began. After he was asked to give a lecture for an organization of businessmen, Ugo began to reread *Overlord* by Max Hastings and *The Longest Day* by Cornelius Ryan, inspiring what was to become an overwhelming preoccupation with WWII that culminated in his last monumental paintings. Ugo wrote this that year:

*We had been quartered in our boat for the past two days—
it was night. Tomorrow would be the sixth of June—1944. The day had
been dismal, gray, the usual small talk among the men. Twenty-two
months in England! And now we were leaving. Why did the Regimental
Commander say to us before we boarded ship, "I expect most of you
back in twenty-four hours"? He had hemmed and hawed but that was
all he really said. None of us believed him. I was a member of a team
of forty special combat troops selected from the 29th Division, Military
Police Platoon—and part of the 116th Regiment scheduled to assault
Omaha Beach, a crescent-shaped silvery strand in front of the seaside
villages of Vierville and Colleville—Sur Mer. The attack would consist
of five assault waves; then the main body of troops would begin landing—I would be in the first assault wave. How ironic though: only a few
months ago, I had been transferred from a B.A.R. (Browning Automatic
Rifle) linesman in Company G to the 29th Division M.P. (Military Police)
Platoon. This had been a welcome change—despite the continued rigor-
ous training, my new duties had provided me with a new set of experiences, and I assumed options other than a first-wave assault on Hitler's
Fortress Europe. Much later I realized that irony was only one face of
destiny, and that fate was not subject to human continuance.*

*Sometime during the night—we began to move, slowly at first. Soon the
ship fell to rolling. The men were resting, or sleeping or roving around
on deck. We had ships on either side, and I saw several in a line behind
me—black, flat silhouettes with very small blue lights. One small boat
in front of us seemed to leave a long phosphorescent glow in its wake.
The ship had more movement now—we must have left Portsmouth
Bay more than an hour ago. I felt vaguely sick, restless, and tired—it
was close in the cabin, dimly lit with blue lights. Somewhere the diesel
engine droned on. Lying back in my bunk—I gazed at the silver dollar
resting on my chest—my combat boots—the musette—all in order—I
wondered about these objects, the rifle, the bandoleer of ammunition,
the grenades—soon I would put them on. Sometime later the order was
given; there was a great deal of activity—one by one, heavily burdened*

*men climbed up the narrow steps to the deck. I worried about all the
extra weight, the metal disc signs we were to put up as markers—somewhere along the beaches and roads of Normandy. I was troubled by
the sense of reality, which seemed too much prepared—too staged in
advance—it seemed absurd that all of this had to be invented. Everything had become terribly physical, related to each other mysteriously:
battleship gray, olive drab—all of one purpose—a mask of dull heavy
brown—inane comments and jokes betraying the white vulnerable flesh
beneath—There was that subtle odor—the sweat of anxiety. Whatever
of dread, of honor, was linked to other events, other times, other men
from Troy to the Argonne, was I another victim? An expendable? As
day broke the sky separated from the sea—it was leaden gray, the sea
darker, rougher. The square nose of our boat steadily pounded against
the waves blending with the sounds of diesels and slapping winds.*

*Ahead, just below the horizon, a long gray strip floated between sea
and sky. To my left, and to my right, ships of all sizes appearing like
phantom silhouettes—a muffled booming, insistent and rhythmic
rolled with the winds. At some distance from the closest boats, white
spouts mushroomed from the gray water and turned into black drifting funnels. Like random golf balls, shells had dropped from the sky.
Surprised, disbelieving—while my hand snapped the chinstrap from
its snug position under my chin. (A loose-fitting helmet under artillery
fire was a defensive action.) Something was out there! I was in my
body's space in a protective cocoon of equipment and a vast armada of
ships. The long gray strip grew visible into land, misty, gray, shrouded.
More waterspouts with black plumes—closer now—they seemed futile.
Ahead the land had contoured; from the slow rise of the pale beach
to its heights, it looked exceedingly peaceful, gray, and still. Stretches
of earth or sand dotted with clumps of gray grasses—along the bluffs
outcroppings of rock—at the water's edge a heavy mist.*

*Suddenly something was happening to the land. Great clouds of smoke
and dust erupted from white flashes all along the bluffs and ridges.*

*There was now a fury of sound as the naval bombardment began. Large ships five to six miles at sea were pounding the coastal fortifications. Overhead—the sky boomed and thundered—was cracked and ripped by thundering shells—and the steadily growing roar of fighters and bombers—(above Omaha, 324 bombers were dropping their lethal load three miles inland beyond the targets)—the guns of Omaha Beach remained. Only a half mile or so from the coast the German batteries were untouched—waiting.... We were now less than one mile from Omaha Beach—shells from the fleet still thundered, but the guns along the Atlantic Wall were silent. The coast was looming larger, stretching out and dissolving in wreaths of haze and plumes of smoke drifting down from the bluffs. The stillness was immense—as in a pantomime of movement without sound—in the midst of sound. The world had become immediate and shrunken, gray dreams of grotesqueries.*

*Long bobbing lines of assault boats some veering off their course—as if lost—others sinking lower and lower—some disappearing beneath the waves—To our left, amphibious tanks, their canvas balloons flapping and floundering. Men wading slowly in the deck, some dead, floated gently. It seemed we were gliding now. The craft rose and fell with the swells—five hundred yards—four hundred yards, the guns of Omaha burst the silence.... A new fury of artillery shells and mortar fire swept against the boats—we were moving into this deadly hail—toward the thrashing surf beating over steel and concrete obstacles—poles of steel capped with mines.*

*The beach seemed a dead deserted land. No one moved upon it—the men in the boats were gray shadows listening to the sound of the craft as it butted the waves—heads low, hands gripping rifles, faces gray— everything was gone now but the body—like an animal, tensed, coiled.*

*Less than three hundred yards from the beach now—I could look directly ahead. There was a rising din in my ears. The boat had made a sickening lurch and seemed to float amidst a tangle of steel beams.*

*The diesels roared as it turned—and hung helplessly—impaled. Silhou-
ettes of men huddled tensely along the deck—voices lost in the fury of
wind and sounds. One voice clear—"The ramp is coming down! We can't
move! You've got to swim for it!" The grating of chains—the steel cover,
the square blunt nose of the boat was dropping, dropped a path into the
open sea. There was a moment when the men seemed stunned, unmoving,
automatically I fumbled with the tiny compressor, which would inflate
my life belt. I wasn't sure it would work—I had never used it before—we
had expected to wade from our boats and dash to the shore. Several men
on the ramp—I walked forward, the ramp's edge was below the water. I
just kept walking—until I plunged into the sea. This was deep water—I
was heavy with equipment. The water filled my ears and nose. It was
cold, dark, and silent below. I clutched at my rifle, should I let it go—to*

*free my hands? I felt the water, a shock of cold needles penetrating my clothing and seeping into my skin—a cool slow liquid—it was lifting and rocking me—slowly—I burst to the surface, my hand to my helmet. The heavy sea swells were pushing me. The sea was all around. Fifty, sixty yards ahead was the land. A worm's eye view—my body instinctively moved towards it. I thought of disengaging the strap tightening my shoulders—It had begun to hail machine gun fire skimming the water—a rapid firing of tiny pebbles splashing and zinging.*

# INTRODUCTION

By Maxine Giannini

Perhaps one would expect to really know and understand one's mate of thirty-seven years. What secrets, what silences could there be, after all that time? What hidden events, buried emotions, forbidden topics could be explored? What conversations were lost in the petty pursuit of daily life: the children, the house, the job, the friends, our families, the rush of the holidays, the struggle to survive? How was it possible not to know, and comprehend what happened to you, and to the men of the 29th Division. The chasm that existed between a war veteran and a civilian was enormous, the difference in age—you at twenty-five and in the war, and I, fifteen a teenager in high school—gave us completely different perspectives. Then there was the silence. The unspoken. You were not alone in your silence—it was as if there never had been a WWII, never a D-Day, never the loss of Division after Division, never a Holocaust, just that sweet, boring, mundane, conventional 1950s, '60s , '70s until '93, the year of your death. The world was eager to forget the upheaval and madness of WWII. Of Hitler, Mussolini, Emperor Hirohito, the bomb, Dresden, Auschwitz, we averted our eyes, and the veterans knew that they couldn't reveal what they had seen. A reality so horrific, that it had to be eradicated from one's consciousness, like a nightmare one tries to erase in the early morning light. You used to say to me that I was naïve; I didn't know what life was really like; here in the states, we all were living a dream, and there in Europe, you knew of the nightmare.

That's why you came back. I knew you were here—it was the morning after your funeral, February 3, 1993. I was sitting alone at about two a.m. in the living room, and I sensed your presence.... I know it sounds a little nuts, but you were here, and you made me understand that I had to tell your story, to write the book that you intended to write, and to be sure that the story which is yours, would be told.

On June 6, 1944, Ugo Giannini landed on Omaha Beach at H+70 minutes as one of a platoon of military police assigned to the 29th Division. Ugo's team was assigned the task of controlling the incoming traffic. There were thirty-seven men in his platoon; they were decimated in the first ten minutes. Six men got to the beach. Someone told Ugo that he was needed on the bluff above. He climbed the Vierville Draw, jumped into a crater made by naval bombardment, and spent that day and part of the next as an eyewitness to the greatest invasion ever conceived by the military. Remarkably, he began to draw. These are the only drawings made that historic day, as well as the next.

This book is the story of one man, in the context of World War II; a man who was a poet, an artist, and had the strength of a boxer. A civilian used to the comforts and hysteria of an immigrant Italian family. In love with Rene, his childhood sweet-heart.[1] Plunged into the hell of war.

The letters and the drawings that follow are from those days, June 6, 1944, to June 1945. The language is of that time, the drawings done on the spot, then.

It is through the eyes of this particular eyewitness that we can return to those terrible times, and begin to understand what it must have been like, for just one man to experience war. Perhaps through the individual narrative, we can understand the universal lesson of the brutality of war through the transformative experience that is unique to the infantry soldier—the man who fights the war on the ground.

Ugo's family consisted of Clara, his mother who was an opera singer; Antonio, a simple tailor, who sat cross-legged, in the old manner of Italian tailors; and his three brothers, Richard the eldest by ten years; Walter, a brilliant musician, composer, and the most nervous of the family; and the baby Harold, a strapping, direct, and simple man who worked laying linoleum floors in kitchens. Clara had eleven pregnancies. Four sons survived, and of the remaining pregnancies, one daughter lived only to die in infancy of diphtheria. The family was united by Clara and her wonderful cooking. One didn't want to miss those spaghetti dinners on Sunday or the all-out cooking of the Christmas holidays and Easter. Clara cooked almost every day of her married life, and she cooked for five hungry men. The aromas from the kitchen were astonishing. Ugo had never eaten or even seen peanut butter as a child. He didn't speak English until kindergarten. Walking into the Giannini house in East Orange, New Jersey, was to walk back in time to the medieval village of Serra Capriola in Italy. Life was hard. It was the depression, and the Gianninis moved fifteen times. When Ugo was eleven, he came home from school to find all the furniture in the house repossessed. Only a chair and a small table remained. Clara cooked in an electric coffee pot, and made ersatz meatballs and spaghetti sauce for the family. There was no money for meat.

Ugo worked for the WPA (Works Progress Administration, a New Deal program that put millions of Americans to work during the Depression). He raked leaves and did maintenance work in the local parks. (Pa was unemployed.) He attended the National Academy of Design in New York and worked for a furniture company, illustrating catalogs. He showed enormous artistic talent at an early age and was encouraged by his high school teachers to attend art school. And Ugo was in love with Rene, his childhood sweetheart, his obsession. By the time Ugo was twenty-one in 1940, he had a job in advertising for Sears in Philadelphia, Pennsylvania. Life was taking on a routine and ordinary dimension. There was no way that he could have known that the world as he knew it was on the verge of changing completely, that he would be hurled into an unimaginable war in faraway lands and that his sense of reality would be destroyed forever. The Ugo who left for the war—after being drafted in 1942—would never return. The man who returned from the war was unrecognizable to Clara, and she said, "What have they done to my son?"

There was a huge disconnection between the civilian population in the United States and the men who fought the war—almost a conspiracy of silence. The news of the war was limited, and the letters from the GI's were censored—no mention of places, times, battles, or deaths were permitted. An unreality between what Ugo was experiencing and what he communicated in his correspondence became apparent. As Ugo tried to hold onto his memories of his family and Rene and freeze them in time, his family had no idea of the violence of war—of what terror and danger, what anguish, deprivation, and horror was the daily bread of their son. As Rex Potts, Ugo's sergeant said, "I didn't have the words. Besides, who cared?" This said fifty years after the war was over. The rupture between war and civilian life would be complete and endure for the rest of Ugo's life.

The mystery and secret world of war would create an abyss between soldiers and civilians. After the war, the veterans of the 29th Division returned to their families as strangers in a strange land. The not-so-subtle indoctrination into the military, the months of combat, the strain of being shot at, bombed, having their comrades killed on a daily basis tore at the foundation of everything they learned prior to being inducted into service. How to set all this aside and pretend that it didn't exist. The silence of the veterans was almost universal.

During the war Ugo's mother wrote to him in Italian; he answered her in English. In his closet, in a neat stack, I found about thirty letters. They were tied with a blue ribbon. Ugo's mother had saved the correspondence. It was customary for the Giannini family to save letters of every description. Ugo retained all his correspondence from World War II. The written word was precious and documented the physical and emotional experiences. There was something more—Ugo had expressed a desire to become a writer; perhaps these letters would be valuable to him in the future.

Ugo and I met in 1951. I was twenty and he thirty. Mrs. Husserl, my piano teacher, mentor, confidant, and inspiration introduced us. Her home was a place that felt European, filled with music, books, sculptures. There were refugees arriving from Hitler's Germany, musicians, and intellectuals. There were wonderful conversations, almost a salon ambience. Mrs. Husserl took a personal interest in her students. She had a profound influence on me. She pointed the way professionally by having me teach music; she changed my destiny by introducing Ugo to me. He had returned from Paris after studying art with Fernand Léger. I didn't know of his war experiences, nor did I have any idea of the effect that the war had upon him. Battle fatigue was rarely discussed and post-traumatic stress disorder was unheard of.

Nor did I know of his love for Rene. After we knew each other for a while, we discussed his former girlfriend at length. It was such an unresolved and tangled affair. The aftermath left him spent and disillusioned. Something had happened between the family and Rene while he was in the service. They were convinced she wasn't the person Ugo perceived her to be. To Ugo's astonishment, he began to receive malicious mail from his mother, Evelyn (his sister-in-law), and Richard (his brother). A series of letters began between him and Rene. No single event could have a more devastating effect on him. The war, the separation, the bitter family interference were all so destructive that they couldn't survive as a couple. But in a tragic way, Ugo couldn't let go. I felt sorry for her and sorry for him.

The past was over, or was it? Ugo used to say to me, "What are you doing with me? An artist, unemployed." He didn't want to have children. "There is too much suffering to bring anyone else into this world."

I didn't want to continue our relationship without the hope of marriage and children. Ugo had decided marriage wasn't for him. I was young and unwilling to suffer. I loved him totally, but the complexity and ambivalence of our relationship was unbearable. I left for Europe for three months. I asked Ugo not to meet me when I returned. I was willing to sever our relationship. If however, he felt he was ready for a commitment to share our life, fine. Otherwise, I asked him to please let me go. We met at the boat in Hoboken. We married in 1955. Laura was born in 1957 and Mark in 1960. Ugo had a studio where he painted and gave some art classes. I taught piano. Somehow we survived. In 1965, Ugo became a professor at Caldwell

College in Caldwell, New Jersey. This was based on his studies at the Art Students' League in New York City and with Fernand Léger in Paris.

We bought a house in 1961. Ugo put his personal belongings in the basement, having been told by the previous owner that the basement was dry. The next week we had a major flood. Ugo was terribly upset and went about drying and restoring a ton of "stuff." The studio was one of the two master bedrooms in our house. After Ugo died, I found the letters. That "stuff" he dried was the complete correspondence between Ugo and Rene. When they had broken up, she returned all of his letters to her as well as all her letters to him.

I broke my hip in the summer of 1996. In August I began to read the correspondence. The letters are very beautiful and at the same time quite appalling. They express a torrent of emotions and truly document a period. They are a historical record of a WWII GI.

I'm not quoting the entire letters. The extremely personal I'm omitting, and I am not using the actual name of the former girlfriend. The letters reveal the effect of WWII on one soul, from D-Day to V-Day and beyond and not only the physical and spiritual duress, but also the epiphany. Many times Ugo told me he knew how things really were. He knew the truth of existence. Had Ugo's family understood what Ugo was enduring, they would have refrained from their negative letters. Had Rene understood, she might have been less demanding. As it happened, the war brought out destructive emotions, all in the name of love.

Walter, Ugo's older brother, gave me a group of letters in 1997. These letters date from 1942 to 1945. These two brothers were closest in philosophy than other members of the family. Ugo was also very protective of Walter—a kind of role reversal. Walter was "high strung," emotional. He seemed to rely on Ugo for strength and steadiness. Harold, the baby, was in the war. They subsequently met in Germany.

I believe these letters are a testament of what it was to endure WWII as an infantryman, and I believe that Ugo would want to share his story with the world, lest we forget.

---

1. Rene is not the correct name of Ugo's sweetheart. I changed the name to protect her privacy in the event that she is still living.

# Chapter One

# JUNE 1944: H-HOUR

## AGONY AT VIERVILLE

The drawing *D-Day, H-Hour+7, Vierville-sur-Mer* depicts the first moments of landing. A self-portrait: helmet still on his head, the yin and yang sign of the 29th Division showing through the water on Ugo's sleeve and helmet, rifle clutched, terror on his face, his buddy hit on his right side, then another on his left, equipment floating, next to the German Obstacle with the Teller mine. The German General Rommel had the beaches fortified with thousands of these obstacles for just such an event.

In 1997, I contacted two of the members of the MP special platoon, Rex Potts and Dom Russo, who landed with Ugo. Rex, by that time an old man, wept when he heard my voice. He was Ugo's sergeant. He told me that he had never discussed the war with anyone—not his sons, not his wife. When he returned home he thought *who would be interested?* It was a terrible strain for him to speak with me—fifty years after June 6, 1944. He said of the thirty-seven men on the boat that only six were alive after the first ten minutes. He had dashed to the right, while Ugo had gone to the left. When did they meet again? I don't know. Dom Russo told me Ugo was his best man at his wedding. I didn't know that. But why would I? I was twelve years old when the war began. Dom was in another landing craft, on a special mission to Le Percée. The mayor had been in contact with the American forces. Dom and four others rushed to Le Percée in order to save the mayor, but it was in vain. The collaborators had hanged him in the square. Dom said that Ugo was close to the headquarters of General Gerhardt (the Commanding General of the 29th Division) most of the time, and that he did artwork for the 29th, including traffic signs. Ugo had never talked about this.

In 1944 there were no old men with aching memories, only the immediate experience. Ugo jumped into the water and got to shore. Someone came to him and said an MP was needed on top of the bluff. When he climbed the hill he found himself completely alone. He jumped into a bomb crater, where he began to draw the battle scene as it unfolded before him.

*Omaha Beach, June 6, 1944*

*Dog Green, the MP Combat Team, was scheduled to land during the operation of the underwater team while breaching paths through mines and underwater obstacles. This sketch depicts the beach and obstacles moments before landing.*

*D-Day, June 6, 1944.*

*D-Day Plus 2*
*[June 7, 1944]*

*I retraced my way from the battered remains of Vierville-sur-Mer. I*
*walked slowly, dragging my unwilling soul with me and forcing it to*
*inhale the death odor.*
*I was alone, searching for my comrades—37 men who were hurled*
*ashore yesterday morning. (Or was it years ago?)*

*I walked, stopped, resumed again always against the visible signs of*
*war. Which way did it go?—I reached the first enemy machine gun*
*emplacement. Leaned heavily against its sand bags. They were vomit-*
*ing their white dusty guts—It was still—very still—but I heard the war*
*crashing, exploding in my ears, my nose, and my mouth. I drew from*
*a smashed wet pack of cigarettes—the bitter nicotine tasted sweet—I*
*inhaled thick quantities of smoke like vaporous balls of opaque*
*cotton—I wanted to forget, to stop thinking or feeling—I wanted to rest*
*or to die—a thin plaster of white mud, darker brown where it was still*
*wet, painted my legs, my boots, my hands and—yes—it must have been*
*inside me too, in my stomach and along—*

*D-Day + 2: looking out to Pont Du Hoc. Coming down the bluff, only bodies piled as far as he could see.*

They have sent me – their hacked bodies

are limb less; maggots feed on their tongues

– In their gaping mouths

– In their hollow eyes Death feeds!

They have sent me – to tell you that Death feeds

on them – whom you loved!

They want to tell you – – – – they forgive you

They sent me thus – one of them and pieces of all of them

And the strength of their forgiveness Giving me life – to tell you this.

They said "We forgive you" – – – – – – – – – and then they died

From them – – – – – – I picked myself up

    Out of them – – I singled

Limbs, arms, feet, body and head

    I stood naked on the beach

And I was no one – – but I was all.

They have sent me – and I have

Found you – – to tell you

They forgive you – – – – – –


Upon returning to the scene of Omaha D + 2


    Day has passed, and half the night

    Still I linger here, on this rock – – – – – –

    Below the seething sea sings and bright

    Demons dance where a burning moon

    Sinks its silver substance into the sea

    "One step forward and below

    Sings the wind" There lies eternity

*June 14, 1944*

*My own,*

*There are a few things a diary could contain that I do not insert in my
letter to you—These things will be with me in a part of my memory
I wish to destroy—I will not talk of them, since the idea of their existence—even now is unreal with horror—so do not ask for a description
that I labor to wipe from my mind.*

*June 22, 1944*

*My Dearest,*

*I've been in France already [deleted by censor] and for more than one
month previous to leaving England I've received no word of you—I only
hope that this delay in mail is due to the postal difficulties—I dare not
think that you may be indisposed to writing.*

*I myself have been unable to correspond and because of this I feel a
sudden drop, as tho' writing letters has become a thing of the past.*

*There are hardships that must be endured, this you know. And I won't
say any words that can fitly describe—nor do I wish to, these circumstances. Only now more than at any time before I spend time consuming every little memory of you.*

*June 28, 1944*

*Dearest,*

*Your letter of May 23 arrived today, your first since my arrival in France—It is not a letter; it is a voice, warmly human, it is a great calm descending upon the storm—it is for me, a moment reborn from some lost eternity. It is you—the fierce throbbing concept breathing light and joy and reason, where there is only madness. Oh but I must check my pen—for it would describe a circle wherein is caged the beast of war.*

*Together, we left England on June 6, and you were with me, in the water, on the beach and through the days and nights—that followed. There were others like me, only they are still forever! And their beloveds wait for words that will not come—Did they not wish some last word to be heard from their blanched lips? Who was there to see and feel their pain? Where was the help they so needed when with their body and shocked brain they lay there, drenched, overcome and dying!—and could you know, would you know that I exposed, felt the presence of a strange lure—it was there that the living and dying all for that terrible hour knew the ugliness of death—and this, note, it was not fear that prevailed, but a resigned waiting for the moment that would leave one crushed and limp. There would not be escape—but there was at least till today.—Yes you are here, your name is the only prayer I ever knew—so believe, accept my spirit—and be conscious that it is much more than love between us—it is, and you know, one soul living in two bodies.*

*Before I forget—please send me as much candy as you can get, this I can distribute among the ragged children. The state of life here is by far worse than that of England.*

*The retreating Germans loot each farmhouse of its cows and blankets and the people are left homeless and hungry. It is common to see a family carrying its only possessions on their backs. They all wear wooden shoes—I managed to buy a pair, I'm sending home. I always had a fancy for them.*

*The Germans have been told that if they surrender to us, we would shoot them. So they fight fanatically to the last.*
*I'm beginning to grasp a bit of French—this breaks the monotony— send me also a French phrase book. (PS)*

*Goodnight and write real soon*
*Forever*

*June 28, 1944*

*Dear Walt!*
*I suppose you have only to read the newspapers and you will know where I am and how I'm doing.*

*Frankly—I've just about had all I ever want of this—I think sometimes how you would react if you were in the Service. I'm certainly a far cry from the person I used to be—someday I'll gain myself, the peace that has been lost for more than two years. I don't know where Harold[1] is yet.—I hope he remains in England a while longer.*

*Received a letter and a V-Mail from you. Thanks. Send my best to Jo[2] and love to all.*

*Sincerest memories.*
*I remain,*
*Ugo*

June 1944

THE WAVE

I grieve now—to behold its ebbing

slipping, washing back, rushing,

—me leaving—forever leaving

I stand now—marooned on the ledge

Hopeless, powerless, voiceless while the sedge forms, twists,

thickens, clings to the edge

The sedge rooting itself, sperm-like growing

Over the ledge, gathers itself, flinging slime or tears on me, now

overflowing I feel now—in the eternity of a moment

The remembered ecstasy of yesterday

The dying despair of today The forward surge The washing back

of me spending and being spent

1. Harold, the youngest of the four brothers, was stationed in England with a top secret division, which was designed to deceive Hitler's High Command into thinking the main invasion was to occur at the Pas-de-Calais, the nearest French town to England.
2. Jo, Walter's first wife.

# Chapter Two

# JULY 1944: REQUIEM ST-LO

## NORMANDY, FRANCE

In July the 29th Division was engaged in fierce fighting; the objective St-Lo. There was a stalemate, and the American forces were unable to push forward. The Generals, Omar Bradley and Eisenhower, were frustrated and devised a plan called Operation Cobra. The 29th Division was scheduled to head the attack; they were opposed by crack German troops. The strongest of the German ground forces were the Paratroops. General Eisenhower stated: "With an authorized force of 16,000 men and a larger allotment of machine guns than the normal infantry divisions, the parachute troops were the best of the Germans for stout resistance on an extended open front." The 29th had been in continuous battle since the June landing, and were by then battle-hardened troops. St-Lo occupied a critically important position and had to be taken at all costs. The costs ended up being extreme; the Germans lost 97,000 men in three weeks, averaging 2,000 to 3,000 daily. (*The Long Line of Splendor*, 1742–1992).

The portrait entitled *Memories of St. Lo* catches the psychological impact of war. The young American civilian has been transformed into a battle-weary "Old Man." Men coming into the 29th as replacements, who had not experienced battle, recognized the veterans with their vacant stare, their lack of enthusiasm, and their quietness. How long did it take to become an "Old Man"? From June 6, 1944, to July 18, 1944, or from D-Day until the fall of St. Lo, the men of the 29th served continuously. In June, 4,686 of their men were killed, wounded, or missing in action—another 4,448 in July. Was that enough? More than half of a division? Ugo stated in a letter of July 9, 1944: "To those at home the war is a gradually deepening form on the surface of a map, but to those of us here—there is no miracle but the price is paid."

*Memories of St. Lo,*
*an old man of war*

"On the 18th of July, 1944, The Commanding Officer, Capt. Vern E Johnson, and 15 enlisted men, attached to special Task Force Charlie, took part in the capture of, and occupation of St. Lo. This detachment remained in St. Lo for a period of three days, leaving on July 20, when Division moved into rest area." Vern E. Johnson was the C.O. of the Military Police platoon. He survived the war and in the 1980s contacted Ugo. Task Force Charlie (1) was a motorized, heavily armored force, which occupied St. Lo after severe house-to-house combat.

1. "Charlie" is the army designation, used in the transmission of messages for the letter "C"; in this instance "C" denoted Brigadier General Norman D. Cota, commander of the task force.
(Maryland in World War ll. 1950)

*July 3, 1944*

*Dearest,*
*Just received your long delayed package. It took two months in arriv-*
*ing—but at a most opportune time—everything in it I need except of*
*course the cigarettes.*

*—Say that chicken was it! I made a hot soup and added a bit of*
*pepper: You can never quite imagine how good it was. I confess, I bare-*
*ly realize the primitive tenor of this existence.*

*In fact, comforts are a strange, thing, which one can do very nicely*
*without. I could expand a bit on how we live here but I'm sure you*
*would accuse me of deserving sympathy—ha! ha!*

*However foot powder is a fine thing to have, especially when one*
*doesn't have the benefits of a bath or one hasn't removed socks or shoes*
*for almost a month.*

*Say—How about dropping a few more letters in the box this week?*
*It gets very lonely here you know:*

*Until later*
*Goodnight*
*As ever yours*


*July 5, 1944*

*Dearest,*
*Thinking as I am, and toying with so diversified a selection of subjects I*
*feel prompted to give order and shape, despite time and fate's skeptical*
*attitude towards fulfillment.*

*You and I both, are living and have lived since our separation on the*
*hope, that is almost knowledge, that we shall once more and for time*

*to come, meet and prolong that reunion for, in fact, to the ends of our destinies. I feel positive that the scheme of things for us is only an embryo and the tomorrow is designed to outweigh with its bright hopes all the sadness and horror of the past....*

*There is another phase I meant to speak of—namely that, for more than two years I have struggled to keep from floundering in the cesspool of this mob-existence or mobile concentration camp. It has not been easy— devoid of intellectual pursuits—devoid of culture and the things—to me which were life, to keep from sinking below the level of decency and to avoid the vast vacuum which would absorb all individual thought.*

*The best of me then, or at least, what you knew of me can be found only in these notes to you. This may account for that peculiar "reserve"—I guard with increasing vigil the scattered leaves of yesteryear, and patiently day and night I gather them close———I have then the collector's priceless jewels.*

*Do I sound detached from the idea of war? But why should I burden you with the fury of its sound and sight? I shudder at the impulse that would plant in your mind a vivid portrayal of it.*

*Operation Cobra, St. Lo, July 18, 1944.*

*If you would have the news—I can brief its highlights for you. Our outfit received the presidential citation (big deal!) This far the initial assault on that gray day—more news? Sorry but it's "Verboten" ha! ha!*

*July 7, 1944*

*Dearest,*

*I admit my patience is turning sour on me. I receive far too little correspondence from you. And if it pleases you to make me happy you will look into this sad matter—I'm trying desperately to understand and project myself in your place—but I fail to reason why you allow days to slip by and with them the word I wait for day by day. It angers me to think that my mail appears always reluctant to come.*

*Everyone is receiving mail quite regularly again—but me! Am I indeed forgotten? The last I heard from you was May and here it is July 7.*

*Please overlook this complaint if you know that I shall soon be rewarded with letters that have gone unfortunately astray....*

*Somewhere in France*
*July 9, 1944*

*Dear Walt!*

*Oho! I have not written to you at an earlier date, rarely have I forgotten you. I was content with idea that the recent letters I dispatched home have somehow passed on to you. Letters received from home indicate that no one imagined I was ever to leave England on the business of war. This I observed with a mixture of gratitude and surprise. Perhaps it is best you remain ignorant of my circumstances. There can be nothing gained in the telling of them. I'm sure my life here would intrude violently upon your own. The difference is so great! My sole complaint, and I honestly believe it not to be insistent, is that letters for me arrive rarely and far between. I am deeply concerned for Harold, and yet I hear nothing from him nor do I have his address.*

*The only consolation is a very strong presentiment that suggests this year as being decisive to the end. And if this is not to be fulfilled, at least I'm happiest in believing that it will.*

*To those at home the war is a gradually deepening front on the surface of a map—but to those of us here, there is no miracle but that the price is paid. Contemplating the thought that someday this madness will be a thing of the past is a strange thought, for in the memory of some it will never die—and I confess, personally, I view with a feeling of uncertainty that civilian life can ever be a returning. Too much has happened to ignore its influence on the future. And I do not understand the ceremony of drums and flags and parades as indicative of anything but a horrible rejoicing where there should be mourning instead.*

*—I'm glad you realize the folly of struggling to achieve. It is best to work unconscious of the word success—herein lies achievement. Every hour, every day can be an attainment measured only by the happiness resolved from it. Life is not so long that we can afford to ignore its simple pleasures.*

*How is Joann? And are you happy in your studio? Please send me a more informative letter, even if it suggests gossip. I'm dying to know about the many little things and the people I used to know.*

*Just received a most savory package from home and a letter from you—this most encouraging—tho' in all modesty I am feeling quite confident. "Now then," as old MacMurray used to say: "All for the interest of science!"*

*As ever,*
*Ugo*

*29th Division, St. Lo Sector, prisoners of war, St. Lo 4 km.*

July 27, 1944

My Dearest,
Have you forgotten me? Then why do you not write? I live in vain for
your letters—but they do not come, to bring me either joy or sadness.

Since landing—I have received two letters, one dated as far back as
May 23rd and the latest one dated July 1st. This one I am grieved to
say I lost, tho' I have the picture of you in my wallet.

I have not been writing of late except to the folks—reason of which I
will not discuss.

Perhaps you are ill? I pray not. I am much too tired to stress the urgency with which I need word from you—However if you insist on silence,

*I am not responsible for my misery of mind and heart, and I can no longer control a despair that has left me to think and feel only the emptiness—the damnable darkness of existence.*

*All my faith, all my hope I placed in you, and you do not respond. I wish you to know that I will not forget this, and you will remember these fifty days of silence. You are growing away from me—do you know?*

*Are you happiest in forgetting? Only let me know.*

*Goodnight and may you have the kindness to write, at least once a month.*

*Chapter Three*

# AUGUST 1944:
# HEDGEROW COUNTRY

## VIRE, FRANCE

In August of 1944, the 29th Division began the pursuit of the German Army through Normandy. The Germans intended to fight a delaying action through the Hedgerow country. The roads were mined; trip wires were placed at field entrances; tanks and self-propelled guns were used in order to slow the Americans. (*29 Let's Go*) There was no sleep—the 29ers were continually harassed by machine guns.

On August 1, 1944, Tessy-sur-Vire fell. Vire was the city Eisenhower said was the pivotal point on which the American Army would swing. The hedgerows were dense, ancient barriers, hundreds of years old, which made each field a killing ground. The Germans utilized these natural barriers as ideal cover for machine guns, as well as mines and booby traps. Vire had been under continual artillery fire, as well as being bombarded by American bombers on D-Day. Leaflets had been dropped over the city warning the civilians of the bombing, but had landed in a nearby forest. One leaflet was brought to the French official, who was a collaborator with the Germans. He chose not to inform the citizens of Vire. When the people of Vire saw the American planes they hailed them, even though hundreds were killed by their bombardment. Ugo was astonished at the French villagers who welcomed the Americans with open arms, even though their cities had been leveled to the ground.

Vire is on high ground bounded by the Vire River and with three hills west and south of the river. Hill #219 was captured and cleared by the 116th Regiment, 3rd Battalion, on August 5, 1944. Robert Grande of the 115th described it this way:

*We had met slight opposition but it wasn't anything that would hold up for more than thirty minutes. Our two squad platoon had just finished clearing a farmhouse and was ready to take off for the next hedgerow. When all Hell broke loose. We got two feet beyond our hedgerow, Pvt. J Foley, asst. squad leader was the first one to get it—right between the eyes. I saw his knees buckle under him. Sgt. Potter, leader of the 1st squad, Weaver and Sparks were pinned down before they could get over the hedgerow. The 1st Platoon on the left, was also pinned down, so we twelve men reached the next hedgerow with our left flank exposed to machine-gun fire and sniper fire.*

*We had no sooner reached the next hedgerow when we realized that we were being picked off, one by one. We shifted our fire from the direct front to the left flank. I saw Weaver bring his rifle to his shoulder, but he didn't quite make it, and a Jerry bullet got him. Sgt. Afanasewicz, 1st Squad leader, was fifteen yards down the hedgerow with a BAR. (Browning Automatic Rifle.) American infantrymen cherished the BAR . it was a hybrid designed to have the portability of a rifle, but the firepower of a machine gun. Every twelve-man rifle squad had a single BAR.' (Beyond the Beachhead, J. Balkoski. p. 84). He was on his last magazine so he called to Young for some more ammo. Before Young could reach him he saw, and so did I, the smoke from the bullet that got Afanasewicz directly between the eyes. Young then began crawling back to me. He was pretty excited, and said that everyone had gotten killed except the two of us, which was quite true.*

*I was about to tell him to lie down and play dead when a burst of machine-gun fire got him in his gut. He fell by my side, and I pulled him closer to the hedgerow and told him to be still. He called for a medic a couple of times before he realized that it was impossible for a medic or anyone else to reach us. I told him to start praying, which was what I had been doing since I hit the hedgerow. I told him that we'd have to play dead until the darkness came, and that was eight hours to go. I was in such a position that my legs began to get numb, but I was scared to move.*

*Young became conscious again and told me that he was going to die. I made believe I was mad as hell at him, and told him that a good Texan never dies. That brought a weak grin from him and he went back into another state of unconsciousness.*

*Just before dark I saw Private Tregembo, who was five yards or so away from me, began to stir. I whispered to him and he turned his head to me. I crawled over to him and he pointed to his legs. I nodded and whispered to him to take off all his equipment. As soon as both of us had done that I started to drag him as best I could. When we had gotten about fourteen yards from the hedgerow I suggested a rest. His legs were paining him too much so I told him to crawl as best he could while I tried to go back for a stretcher.*

*I was about twelve feet from our hedgerow when a guard halted me. I told him who I was and he told me to advance with my hands over my head. I did so and he let me come through. He took me up to the company CP and there Lieutenant Gentry sent two men to pick up Tregembo. Young was dead. (With permission from J.H.Ewing,* 29 Let's Go*)*

The 29th battle line had moved 5,000 yards by August 15. The Division's combat came to a quiet conclusion by August 16. Orders were now received to prepare for the move to Brittany.

The war in Normandy was over.

For every new location, for every new battle, the 29th trained, reorganized, and analyzed prior battles. The German Army in France was an experienced, highly trained force, who were the invaders and committed to holding their ground. They were unprepared for the tough, brave, and intelligent American soldiers. They were sure the GIs would have neither the stamina nor the pure courage that they eventually encountered. It was not superiority of arms that won the war. It was the resourcefulness and determination of the individual, and the cohesiveness of the Division that prevailed. Because the Germans had invaded France, the French did not consider the allies invaders; they were liberators and were hailed as such throughout Normandy with gifts, flowers, and kisses. Even for the fiftieth anniversary of the Normandy Invasion, the French welcomed the returning American veterans as liberators.

*Portrait*

*August 1, 1944*

*My Own Dearest,*
*For the first time in my life I feel as I have never felt before—your*
*letters of July 17, 18, 19 arrived.*

*Now listen to me, and closely, and remember that I love you with the*
*capacity of this and other worlds. I know the meaning of life and*
*death—believe me! This is why you must abide by what I say. Here it*
*is—There is hope only in life;—only in life will we, can we be togeth-*
*er, after that there is nothing—nothing! Do you understand? Forget*
*what I have said in the past that speaks of other existences. There is*
*only one for us, the thread of which has been temporarily severed, but*
*which every day brings us closer to its repair—that we will continue*

*from there—that we will live again. Look in the mirror. See yourself! And say—"Gogo wishes me to know that I must prepare for his return. (And if he does not return, he begs me to realize that his life is not the beginning nor the end of all things for me.) Tho' I feel it is and I weep and am ill for his safety. He has told me in his own words and his voice was so sure, so clear, almost angry.... I shall be not to death, but to life devoted, for he is the symbol of life."*

*All these weeks without word from you—but I knew you couldn't write; that you are ill, yes I am with sick mind conscious of how helpless I am to you.—and you have been ill since I left what can I do? But say that I feel that this year I'll be home....*

*By every mail I live only for word from you.*

*August 2, 1944*

*My Dearest,*

*Hoping you are receiving plenty of fresh air and sun. And please do not take too seriously my complaint that you are not writing. I know it is quite a task to write when one is ill. I should have known you were not well; perhaps I did, and this I hated to reveal to myself. However, I want you to keep me posted as to your health. Please don't try and conceal from me your welfare—what other interest is there for me? I will take it that you are too ill to write—meanwhile my feelings remain now and forever unchanged for you.*

*I am anxious to learn that you have rested and will continue to do so. How I long to be there beside you. Yet I am grateful that after these two months I can still send letters. There are others who will not write again....*

*I have letters I wrote to you—but I'm a hard censor—so they remain unmailed—at least their contents I can well remember and someday— soon—I shall be delighted to tell you personally of all that has occurred since I left you. Let's just take another breath, grit your teeth and hold on tomorrow is on its way!*

*I must tell you how sweet your last picture was. I have it here in my wallet—(but whose hand is that resting on your shoulder? Or who is the character you blocked out? Someone I don't know?) Don't mind, guess I'm jealous! Ha! Ha! as I've always been of any one near you.*

*Saw my first cinema here in France last week. In an old barn. "Cover Girl," I thought the sight of many lovelies rather breathtaking. I took a fancy to that song throughout—Will you purchase some of the songs I've missed?—records of course....*

*I pray this letter finds you better in health of mind and body and until—next time*
*My life I love you.*

*Gogo*


*August 10, 1944*

*Dear Heart,*
*Although there are hours designated to sleep—there are rude and violent intrusions. The series of which, over so prolonged a period have left their mark—happily enough invisible to the eye, and in the course of time will heal. I am speaking of wounds that bring pain greater than mere physical ruptures. For when the heart is ill, the body is indeed insignificant. What has long since become unbearable I now endure unconsciously, as tho', and indeed existing in this strange half-world.*

*The entire horror of all has been, and this I confess without shame, augmented by the knowledge that you have grown seriously ill. I had prepared long ago—even for death—but nothing can still my heart against this fierce tide of consuming grief for you. All my life I converge on your spirit—all of my reason to live—all my hope to happiness, all my dreams, all the beauty, however transient—all my concept of immortality—all revolves about you—and now you are ill—and from your concealing description, for you do not wish me to know, you do not believe in adding to my burdens here, I have drawn my own image—you have been silent—but that silence has spoken to me gravely and with clear voice....*

*August 1944*

*Dear,*

*Your letter of Aug. 17, arrived today—I pored over its content many times and allowed its tones to vibrate through a part of me that has long since died. I wept inwardly, for your message is a tangible proof that those hours we consumed are not mere memory.*

*—This I know and only this—two feet in front of me is my mirrored self, a steel helmet that holds sweat and mental pain—a shoulder that says: leather and steel on flesh—a back that bears a brown hump and a waist that is manacled with bits of pointed death. Below is the light khaki—growing dark with sweat: and the two eternal pendulums dragging studded boots over a road that will not end.*

*August 14, 1944*

*Last night I shall never forget. I shall remind you with thunder in my eyes and manner that you have failed me.*

*Last night I was ill—as you welled up—and in the fever of my mind I resolved to compose this last letter whose urgency is greater than any I have yet written. It is not I—it is you who have failed to absorb the sincerity in my previous letters ... but to you they are only letters. Lovelorn, mushy and casual—They remain pasted in your scrapbook—mocking your—own senses.*

*A soldier on the front line.*

*Here they are, three of the most unlovely letters ever written arriving in order, Aug. 7, 8, and 10. One who loves me and has faith in me does not write such stinging lines. How can I be blunt yet tender? How can your poor little intellect grasp the idea that tho' I love you more than life I still must teach you what a fool you are?*

*Living with me for so many years I am chagrined that the many times you agreed with my chain of thoughts—now that I have gone—has been in vain. There is no end to my anger and disillusionment—How dare you insult my intelligence? My right to manhood? I resent fiercely your implications that I'm having a "good time with the Mademoi-selles." Little fool! At the front there is only death and horror—no Mademoiselles! Christ how faithless you are!*

*August 29, 1944*

*I don't believe a word of this however—so it's quite hopeless to make me mad—besides if you didn't care I should never express so glibly my personal thoughts. On this 29th day of Aug.... I celebrate by myself the thought that I am still alive—there are indeed few who can say "I am a veteran of the 29th Div." All who have not been killed but wounded have returned into action indestructible until they die, as indeed only two remain in my old outfit.*

*I must feel indeed queer, like a ghost who does not know. Since the first hour of D-Day when I dragged myself like a wet rat ashore—ha! I lead a charmed life—but when will that charm be lost?*

*August 30, 1944*
*[on American Red Cross letterhead]*

*[Rene,]*
*Don't get upset! It's the only paper available! Hello there! What's it like in E O? ... I wonder if all the kids will be grown up when I return, and why? As for me I manage to keep that schoolboy complexion—yup! I never want to be a man—They're funny people with funny ideas. I'd*

*Fallen Hero.*

*be satisfied just taking you to a good movie and holding hands in the dark. Yup! You know ice cream, and some candy (licorice drops) and maybe peanuts with the shell—In fact I've got a lot of surprises for you when I get back—just wait.... Surprises yes but not just things—I mean we're going to make up every day of the war since I left. Is it two years or twenty years? I'm not saying how worried I am for you—but please keep well, that's an order!*

*Do you still listen to "Just Music"? I haven't forgotten the theme—it's got a funny sound. When I hear it I almost repicture those many nights, a dark sweet scented room, a chair, a candle glow from the radio. That's real to me! This isn't now. All those pledges, those looks, your sad eyes catching the quiet light. They are not gone are they? They will return? I'm almost afraid so much happiness isn't meant to be.*
*Well goodnight and don't forget, my life, I love you.*

*Gogo*

*Chapter Four*

# SEPTEMBER 1944: REDUCTION OF THE FORTRESS BREST

## BATTLE FATIGUE

The defenses of Brest had been constructed to withstand attack by land or sea. For miles beyond the city the hedgerows had been prepared for the expected offense. An outer band of defenses consisted of an abundance of strong points, heavy in automatic weapons and self-propelled guns, dug well into the earth, some fortified with concrete and steel, all of them forming a great defensive arc that swept around the city. An inner band of ramparts was modernized with steel pillboxes, antitank ditches, road barriers, and minefields. With months of preparation these positions had become an ultimate in defense. The Brest garrison was estimated to hold approximately 20,000 men, in actuality it comprised nearly 50,000. (pg. 121. *29 Let's Go*)

"Landing on D-Day was a picnic compared to Brest.... Brest received the personal order of Hitler to hold for three months."

The Army's After Action Report of September states:
In September of 1944 the American soldiers of the 29th Division felt the full fury of the German forces. "The backbone of the defense of Brest was entrusted to the excellent soldiers of the 2nd Paratroop Division, who fought, in almost every case, as they were ordered by General RAMCKE: 'to the last man'—figuratively speaking.

In the zone of the 29th Division the 2nd Paratroop Regiment of the 2nd Paratroop, Division, the 852nd Infantry Regiment of the 343 Infantry Division and the 899th Infantry Regiment of the 266th Infantry Division were the main enemy forces. In addition to these, other units of the three divisions, plus a multitude of naval, air force, marine and garrison troops formed a part of the defensive forces of the Fortress Brest. At the commencement of the campaign it was estimated that a total of 20,000 men defended BREST proper and the DAOULAS and CROZON Peninsulas. Actually the number turned out to be approximately 40,000. It was stated that RAMCKE (the Major General of the German forces) had promised HITLER he would hold out until September 20. On 18 September, RECOUVRANCE fell, followed by BREST on 19 September and CROZON on 20 September. This tenacity to hold had permeated through all ranks, particularly among the Paratroopers, although there was no question that the defenders were happy to see the end of the siege when it came.

Defenses: The Fortress of BREST, with its natural, French built and German built fortifications, proved to be the most strongly defended locality yet encountered and was probably the most strongly defended port in the West. Defended localities are shown in the colored sketches to accompany this report—"Defenses of BREST The bunkers and pillboxes were of reinforced concrete, in many cases 9 feet thick. Concrete shelters, concrete CP s and casemates all were impregnable to air and artillery bombardment, and could be taken only after assaulted or surrounded by infantry troops. The final shelter, the Naval School and U-Boat Pens, proved to be a veritable building 150 feet underground, which could not be breached by even the heaviest bombardment." (After Action Report, 6 October 1944)

It was during this time that Ugo wrote:

> *Might as well inject this piece of past history—I had suffered one week of battle neurosis while we gave Brest (France) a work over—the Jerries turned their 300 mm naval guns at us, two landed in my back yard, a huge hunk of shrapnel tore a window in my tent (as if I wasn't getting enough ventilation!) To make matters worse our own P 47s bombed and strafed our area—we had a lot of fun (now that it's over.)*

It's ironic, that the port of Brest was so destroyed as to be inoperable; The Allies had to rely on other ports of entry for their desperately needed supplies. Hitler decimated his best troops, he should have reorganized along the boundaries of

Germany where he could have supplied and supported the troops. It was our good fortune; Hitler didn't listen to his Generals.

Brest was totally destroyed, there were only two buildings left standing.

*September 1, 1944*

*I remember you.... When you were only twelve, sitting there in the window corner, reading some unremembered book. You were a Chinese doll—for there was in the slant of the eyebrow, the style of the hair and the lips always ready to smile, a note of something which brought me far away—and yes, you wore an orange colored sweater.*

*I would have forgotten, and it would not have mattered today but I thought then—her face glowed many times with a confused and almost painful rapture, and her large bright eyes would catch my curious gaze and then———softly dip into the shades of shy melancholy—was it— you did not wish me to share your secret?*

*But I had eyes then, cruel curious eyes and they would not leave you alone. Every day I watched you—until I became ashamed of the desires my curiosity aroused in me.*

*And in turn, it was I who became ill tempered and annoyed—because my own face felt the heat of a similar glow. I did well in concealing from you this torment—yet from my heart I would not destroy the sweet sadness the face of you implanted there—And so we spent the years struggling to conquer and explore the secret that had caused such pain and joy.*

*Did you think to find it in the music of Grieg's Nocturne? Did you forget it in the works of Byron and Poe?*

*September 14, 1944*

*Dearest,*

*I had just finished a note to you and already mailed it—sitting here, lost in a not bright world, musing and lost, when suddenly word from you, little angel—a note of Aug. 28, 29.*

*And only now I stated that I would acknowledge only your letters until that one arrived which you would answer.... Sprinkled with pink powder, and recalling you to me strongly—so that my mind drugged by the months of combat, falls back, back and where the hard shell of me refuses to sway and where I, incapable of tears, feel the spirit of youth weeping healthily within.... Feeling that my body is strong, and the blood red and the spirit restless for you, for you! And only you. I have had companions through death and Hell—only you, only you, and I am alone.... But you will help me to forget the pictures hanging in my mind. I know you will help me.*

*Only recently I gazed out over the sea and I thought I could swim the distance, but I am afraid of water of late, and the sight of a beach holds a strange lure and a violent dread.*

*But I shall be drugged with happiness on the ship coming home, and I will choose to forget the dread. There is enough horror and ugliness in this world without my touching upon it. And so if I seem out of place it is only because my efforts search to embrace beauty.*

*I'll keep the war here with its sights and smells and sounds, and you keep beauty and faith there—preserve it for me I will need it. Yes—it is different where I am—there is no bed but the ground often. In fact for two months I slept in a fox hole and when it rains, it just rains until the sun shines. There is little difference between day and night, for we do not undress to sleep, only occasionally removing our shoes. There is no hot bath—lucky to draw water to drink from some stream or well. There are no luxuries or toilets—the ground suffices. Do I miss the comforts of home? No—because there is something else here which drowns all minor complaints. The silent question, we know is always present, "Will I see the dawn?" You understand I think by this slight description. There I'm carrying on not at all what I expected to say. So I don't know what to write about—it's true. I can only repeat what I have said over and over—wait for me—because soon, soon, this must end. I try as much as humanly possible, every day to outlive the grievous fears. Only lately, I have become inclined to nerves. But they are based on long strain, and I'm sure I'll be feeling fine directly—So goodnight and I hope another letter from you arrives soon—it is my only recreation to answer it.*

*Forever yours,*

*Ugo*

*Ugo in Brest.*

*Capturing Prisoners of War.*

*September 14, 1944*

*Dear Walt,*

*I received your letter of Aug 30—I am indeed happy to hear from you, especially so, since the reading of mail is my sole recreation.*

*I wish I could set my feelings apart from my activities—if only to discuss the many topics, but I am obliged to accept the discomfort of emotion as vitally as the discomfort of living. And so to write would define too clearly a reflection that is at once grotesque and horrible. I assure you I am only human and am beset by the anxieties this life affords to what extent?—Well, one's nature cannot change. But if destiny is willing—I can endure further. I am glad you were home—please visit Mom and Dad more often.*

*I haven't heard from Harold—have you? I almost forget he is here in France—I am forced to forget many things—it would be too much to remember. We just must hope for the best—for a tragic hour brings its own grief.*

*As optimistic as everyone in the States is—I have this to say—the Germans do not give up, simply because they have fanatic leaders who are playing a game of "professional soldiers." And I assure you the shaded area on the map conceals from your eyes many truths. Don't ask me why—but you can probably read in the newspapers things I am obliged to leave out in my letters. I have seen all I ever want to see of war—and now I'm tired and desire only, only to come home—but who knows—I am only a number on file. However, I have a fair chance of returning according to points system. Two years foreign service, my months in combat, major battles engaged in, awards received, all these should carry weight, but let us not forget the clauses attached to this system. Perhaps a sudden miracle out of the dark night of hopeless despair—for this has happened. Let us pin our faith on it. However, I am in excellent health despite the situation, and remember—as long as you have health, there is everything to hope for.*

*My Years in the Service,*
*by Sgt. Rex Potts*

*Le Conquet. Outpost, Task Force Sugar.*

*German Prisoner of War.*

# Chapter Five

# OCTOBER 1944: PARIS

## THE SIEGFRIED LINE

After completing its move from France, the 29th Division assembled in Valkenburg, Holland. Once more, the terrain was completely new, and the war would be pursued in Germany with a hostile civilian population. Hitler declared that every civilian was now a soldier. The 29ers were told to use extreme caution. Vast flat farms of turnips and beets, of small apple orchards separated by small villages, each with a church whose spire became an ideal lookout post for observation of the least movement. "This scene presented a serene and somber picture to the 29th Division soldier. The warmth of the Norman farm lands dissolving into the bleak, ominous autumn of the Rhineland." (*29 Let's Go*)

There were very few of the original 29ers left. General Charles Gerhardt—the commander of the 29th Division since their assemblage in England—used the Division as a battering ram to storm the beaches on D-Day. There was to be no let up, from Omaha Beach to St-Lo to the battle for Brest. The casualties, missing in action, and deaths were staggering: 14,563. The division Ugo had trained and fought with virtually disappeared. Now, after no respite, the 29th began the grim, new task of confronting the West Wall or Siegfried Line. This line was made up of a vast construction of poured emplacements with connecting underground tunnels designed to prevent men and tanks access to Hitler's Germany. They were called "Dragon's Teeth."

*Ugo in Valkenburg, Holland, October 1, 1944.*
*These were Harley-Davidson Motorcycles that were issued to the MPs.*

*Valkenburg, Holland, October 4, 1944.*

*October 2, 1944*

*Dear Mom,*
*Received your letter of Sept 19. Glad to know everyone is well at*
*home—I can say the same for myself. I am sorry I am unable to tell you*
*where I am at the present—however, the day is arriving when there will*
*be no more of this secret stuff. We will all be glad for that.*

*I doubt whether I will be able to see Harold. I'm too far from where*
*he is. Glad to know he is well. He wrote recently, and I was greatly*
*relieved. He sent some kerchiefs and perfume from France? How nice.*
*I was always up there making it possible for soldiers to see France you*
*hear? Ha! Ha!*

*The Siegfried Line, with concrete emplacements called Dragon's Teeth.*

*Give my regards to Ann and everybody else I hardly remember.*

*I don't think it is fair for you to remind me to keep single—you've made me feel as though I do not deserve any happiness at all—would you like me to be an old bachelor?—I guess maybe I will now anyway since I can't find anyone to share life the way I see it. I'm going to be a headache—but soon as I get restless I'll let you know. Things will not be quite the same I imagine and there must be adjustments made. However let us not come to conclusions.*

*I've been in the Brest peninsula—lovely country.*

*I just mailed some articles consisting of two separate packages. Let me know when they arrive. There should be a fourth check coming—glad you received the first three.*

*Only lately I drank enough champagne to fill a bathtub and white wine and plenty of eggs—"I get around." I still have a great appetite and I have cultivated an appreciable thirst for various things.*

*No matter how I live I don't lose any weight, and I've even grown a moustache—will you recognize me? Walter wrote recently—I should send him a letter.*

*Regards to Dick and Evelyn & Jr. and Pop*

*Tell them I am eager to see them all at the earliest date.*

*When?*

*October 18, 1944*
*Somewhere in Germany*

*Dearest,*

*I have waited long for your letter of Oct 10 to arrive—It was to be an answer as I directly implied in my note of Sept 17—The answer is there. I shall quote it and you shall see it again as you wish me to see it. "You cannot help me. I asked you to, hundreds of times, you've disregarded my questions wonderfully and answered negatively, what*

*I searched for, I did not see or feel" and in concluding, "I begged you once to give me the solution for any reason why I should believe in your way of life—you refused."*

*Your letter arrived here in good time—eight days and this is your decision of eight days ago. I rarely receive letters—except a few from the folks—and I write only rarely now. If I may—let me say this—whatever life I lead now is not of my choosing and it has been this way since May 13, 1942. It is a life of hardship, of submission, of repression, of danger, of loneliness, of longing, of great physical and mental anguish—of privation.(The full sense of the word) It is a life tho' you undoubtedly wish to know about from me—I have not dared discuss or describe—I imagined perhaps you might have known without my adding to and confirming. I would retain whatever traces of fine feeling I imagine myself to possess. I am humble to the ground and that you should misjudge me, even as a friend, brings sadness—a sense of eternal loss.*

*You wish an explanation of why you should trust and believe in my way of life—I have forced my love upon you, am I forcing it now?—If you loved me, would you ask in sincerity such a question? My way of life, the inner life which is left me has not altered—it is the same path we both loved before I left—and now that I am gone do you betray that trust? Now that I am left, do you tell me I wove a pattern of false——? about your mind?*

*I was good enough for you then—now that I have suffered you condemn me for being self-centered, cheat, liar, infidel, pagan, trustless?—I do not accept the names in your idea of the words. I only know that I have not changed nor broken my trust. If you did not love then—surely now, if you were to see me I could not inspire you with that Passion.*

*The Thousand-Yard Stare: These sketches of 29ers illustrate the complete exhaustion, the hollow-eyed stare of many too long in battle.*

*October 19, 1944*

*My Dearest*

*I was startled to receive today a cablegram. I had for a moment a strange assortment of fears—I expected the world to cave in, why? I don't know, except maybe, being away for so long; I don't really know. Well it's cold outside, but now I'm warm inside, with the nostalgia of old things—I shall keep it now, your cablegram with its message of urgent affection. I shall reread its simple line and remember how it came to warm me when it was cold and lonely—and it's been so long since I felt this way—I wish, I could hold you close to me—then you would know how I miss you—words wouldn't be necessary then. My birthday slipped by—but all the while your dear remembrance was journeying across sea and land, to me. And now it is here, a little miracle with wings.*

*It seems you are here and that I see the beautiful line your hair makes as it cascades down your shoulders—and the full sensitive lips, the white petal skin fresh as wild flowers—and I know, for I have felt the fires which glow in those sad eyes; once long ago; my one arm could easily encircle your waist—it is so small—and the curve there caused great alarm—as you well remember!! There is a deeper instinct; a primitive one, which surges from depths of longing and repressed desire—but are dead memory, nothing more.*
*Goodnite*

*October 30, 1944*

*Dear Mom,*
*Received your letter of Oct. 17 today. I see by it that everybody is worried as all hell—Now listen—you undoubtedly picture a civilian attitude when you imagine the grimness of war. You forget that I am in tune with whatever I am doing and that this life is not any rougher,*

*than what I have been doing for the past two years. When life really becomes unbearable—I will let you know. Until then, please understand that I have one ambition, and that is to return home.*

*On the contrary—I have ample time to write, but I'm fed up with writing letters. Perhaps you can understand me better if I say that there is more of the hidden primitive quality in man than what most gentle people are willing to admit. I have undergone certain natural changes to better fit me for the form of life we now face. I live in the air—so I don't catch colds. If it is cold, I put my overcoat on, and when it rains I wear galoshes, when I get tired I go to sleep, when I'm hungry I eat. I haven't told you a damn thing of how I live—so why do you allow your fancy to picture the usual mud blood and sweat? If I need anything, I sure will ask for it—Come to think of it maybe a few pairs of woolen socks would do nicely. Size 12.*

*I guess we all feel the same way. To me it is ages since I last saw you and everyone at home. I know I should write more often—somehow I only mail one out of every ten letters. It feels like I keep talking to myself when I do write. Well I know there is little we can do or say—all, all is waiting.I really doubt whether I will be able to see Harold. It's almost hard for me to believe that he is here—someplace. Everything is only some fantastic nightmare without rhyme or reason.*

*I received Walter's letter of Oct. 8. He said he may live in N. Jersey. Wherever he is happiest is best. Sorry, I will not be able to make it home for Christmas. You go right ahead making the usual dinner, and I will remember the night. I'm sorry it's three Christmases like that. Try working from that side of the water to get the old boys home because we are forgotten. I guess maybe those pen pushers don't know what it is like to be gone for over two years and then wind up in the thick of things—A guy gets pretty tired of all the nonsense. I just want a chance to ram it down somebody's throat when I get back, and don't think I won't look for trouble, because I intend to!*

*Please buy all the furniture you wish and save the collectors and Constables for me! If I have to spend a few weeks in the hoosegow, it's worth it, to smear their teeth all over their faces. Freedom is a great thing, providing you use it when you have it. And I'll know when it's mine. Be surprised how much people will do for you if you ask them to forcefully enough.*

*Well perhaps I should give you a list of a few items I could use—maybe I sound like I was pregnant but my mouth is watering for—pickles, peppers, onions, (chocolate with nuts only), sardines, handkerchiefs, woolen socks, oh yes, and send me some butter pecan ice cream, ha! ha!! I'll wait till I get home for eggs, milk, and vegetables.*

*Hello pa! I bet you're listening in too. Do me a favor, haul a load of mud upstairs in my room because I won't feel comfortable otherwise—take the mattress and spring out of the bed and lay some boards across it so I can get some sleep. Ha! It ain't funny. It's the truth. Well goodnite and I'll see you all in my dreams.*
*Send my best to Evelyn, Dick and the "Result."*

*Affectionately,*
*G.I. Joe*

*October 30, 1944*

*Hello—*
*I was really thinking that I might have been home this Christmas; perhaps that gives you an idea of how I view time. And here it is almost Xmas and I know it was a pipe dream. There is a scarcity of pipes now so it's rather difficult to dream another. I'm getting a little anxious for the future—the joker has been in hiding for a long time-—and last night I suddenly thought I saw its leering face. Not pleasant! So maybe it's a*

*good thing after all to have left so long ago. It's like an anesthetic maybe. I would like something from you—I don't know what, just something to remind me that it wasn't a pipe dream—the past. I'm over the first glow, and the second is more quiet, that is as strong but not so vociferous.*

*Happy Birthday! I wish I would be there ... I feel empty; a shell whose emptiness echoes the sounds of many places, many longings but it is only a shell.*

*Write me a little note—be surprised how it would warm up the chill. Sure, sure, you want me to tell you that everything is all right. From my side of the fence, it is. How about yours? You never did say when and if you ever convalesced from your previous indispositions.*

*If anybody is going to meet either in this or another world, you can say definitely "I've got an Appointment with Gogo there; In sweetness or in fire he'll be there—he wrote it in my heart, long ago. So I'll live and wait." I am not sure that destiny has been favorable in sparing me thus far—there were others I knew with more reason to live than I. They are gone, even before they experienced the terror of waiting. I am sorry if I whipped up a storm of ungrateful remarks in my last letters. Whatever it is I say, whatever reproach or display of anger, it is only because I wish to do good, to guide you, but not to be cruel no never in the spirit of real anger.*

*Goodnite*

*P.S. I mailed you a small bottle of perfume. I had no choice, there were only three to select from—more as a memento, purchased under the Eiffel Tower in Paris. I was fortunate to be able to convoy our outfit through Paris. I was there only one hour. I left with the impression that it was the most beautiful city I had ever seen. Someday you shall see it.*

*[No date]*

*Dear Walt,*

*Received your V mail of Sept 23 and letter of Sept 20. Nice long, complete letter I thought. Please try and forget about Harold and myself for a while—you'll worry I know, anyway, but just a word of consolation. I am in the best of health, and don't worry about me. If I get wet feet they've been wet many times and nothing's happened. I do not expect you to strain yourself trying to write either music or letters at this particular time. Just be calm about the whole thing—it's wisest. Obviously your letter suggests to me that the city stifles you and that Joann is an impediment to your happiness. I suggest: you come home more often with or without her—and if, as you say you find it difficult persuading her to bend to your ideas—come home without her. Your particular nature demands a woman who is all love not all Intellect. Think this over.*

*Don't make an issue of this thing—she either loves you or doesn't. You come first in her eyes or you do not. I would not be satisfied with in between.*

*I still claim one must eat a bushel of salt with ones fiancée—but then again marriage is only a paper. Easily destroyed—love is indestructible. Don't knock yourself out thinking about it—either you're happily married or you're not happily married. And if marriage is going to decide negatively for your important decisions, why just unmarry yourself.*

*I received a letter from Evelyn today which I must answer shortly. I guess everyone feels about the same all over. I'm in Holland at the present hour. I stopped in Paris for about an hour. The only place in Europe I should really like to revisit someday. It is the most beautiful city in the world—maybe I'm combat happy, or hedgerow crazy, but it was like entering paradise after all those days of savage living. We rolled though however into Belgium, and now I'm here looking for more trouble and getting it.*

*Well let me know when they declare some sort of Armistice—this thing is beyond me. I'm only a soldier and soldiers only fight wars they don't make them. Or end them. Well, give all my love to Rene, if she accepts it—let me know because will I be surprised!*

*And don't forget to remember me to Joann and Mom and Pop.*

*How is the old boy? Younger than ever?*

*Goodnite*

*G.I. Joe*

*Alias Ugo*

*On October 4, 1944, the 3rd Battalion, 116th Infantry, was attached to the 2nd Armored Division and given the mission of teaming with that organization as Tank-Infantrymen to enlarge the gap through the Siegfried Line.*

*Chapter Six*

# NOVEMBER 1944:
# ROER RIVER TO JULICH

## FORGOTTEN HEROES

The men of the 29th Division were faced with the challenges of crossing the Roer River in order to capture Julich. But before they could do this, there were a dozen small German towns that had to be taken. Each town had become a point of resistance linked by lateral trenches to the adjacent towns, most of them able to give each other mutual support across the flat plain of the Rhineland. In addition, the weather in November was the wettest in years; twenty-eight out of the thirty days had rain. The men in foxholes stood knee-deep in mud. Another D-Day was planned, and General Gerhardt's secret message was, "It's a Democratic landslide," which indicated the attack was on. Twenty-two divisions and 500,000 men were employed to crack the Siegfried line before the onset of winter. (After Action Report.) The language of the After Action Report used terms such as "jump off," "button up," and "cleaning up," as code for the astonishing efforts by the 29th Division. "Jumping off," meant that you were on the attack, amidst mines, artillery, and enemy, nowhere to go but forward into the hell of war. "Button up" usually indicated that very little progress was made on the front, and it was time to regroup and dig in for the night. "Cleaning up" meant hand-to-hand combat with the remnants of the retreating enemy.

The battle for Koslar was an immense struggle. It was rare in the After Action Reports for the writer to express much emotion, usually delivering a dry report of ground lost or gained and men wounded, lost, or killed in statistical terms. But in describing the action of November 26, 1944, he stated: "Mere words cannot paint the picture contained in the downright and utter bitterness of the battle that raged on the front of our 1st Battalion this day. In fact, it raged with such fierceness and reached such a feverish pitch at one point that it was hard to believe that a man could live through this veritable inferno."

*November 1, 1944*

*Dearest Heart,*
*After almost two months of wallowing about in mail bags, your letter*
*of Sept. 12 arrived. I enjoyed the snapshots very much. I am aware that*
*you have grown into a young woman. And despite what you may say or*
*imagine, you appear quite healthy. This is as it should be.*

*Musing here—I realize with painful shock that I have been subject*
*to the unsound reasoning of a forced existence. And I shift equally*
*the blame to your own lack of faith in me. It appears that it is not*
*enough for a perverted destiny to separate us, but that we must add*
*self-inflicted grief to that already miserable state. You plague me with*
*your pettiness, such as observing that I write "dearest" after the letter*
*is completed. This is only a habit peculiar to me. Why do you look for*
*nonexistent loopholes? Why must I always be faced with suspicion? Is*
*this the extent of your faith? You ought to be ashamed of yourself! If it*
*is my fortune to return we shall see who is going to blush with shame.*
*But I think I'm always to blame fundamentally. I started out on this*
*campaign long ago.*

*This is hardly the time for pleas of forgiveness—I'll not ask for any. But I*
*will say you and I better snap out of it. Or is there someone else? I think*
*crazy things sometimes all because you have been waiting so long—and*
*I too! Oh it can't be! Rene, Rene what is the matter with us?*
*We don't mean a word of it—all we do is torture each other. As tho' spit-*
*ing the indifferent Heavens. It is we who suffer—not the world! I insist*
*on writing—I'm not dead. I love you deeply; all I ask is a time to come*
*home, only one hour to tell you that I'd rather die than leave you again. I*

*don't remember what I have said in my letters—but if you thought some passages beautiful—they are only a meager expression of the thing you inspire. Do you not see this as the truth? You must! There is no room for doubt. Won't you write to me in the spirit of other days and with hope for the future at this moment, writing is so utterly futile. I must wait so long for an answer. I'm afraid you have ceased caring for me. And life makes no difference now. But as long as you are there I must think! Think! I have forgotten what it is like to be told "I love you," and I'm afraid I haven't said it either in ages. Write to me. I need your help—please write to me. There is no time, there is no time! I need to know now.*

*I'll be standing there and thinking you will not come to me—you will not have my arms about you. I'll just be standing and you will say a faint "hello." Maybe you would not recognize me! And I would walk to you and ask if you are looking for someone you turn and say yes— I'm waiting, but he hasn't come—he should have been here, but I can't see him and I won't know what to say, standing there like a clown. I don't know how much there is left of time—but it leaves only anguish and loneliness which nothing can destroy, only you. I am waiting, for your help, please write to me. It is more urgent than I can say in words—tell me, tell me you are waiting as you used to.*

*Goodnite*
*Duchenka*

*November 3, 1944*

*Dearest,*
*There are many things I am able to tell you now, but I have a "disciplined pen," and it does not recognize readily a newly acquired freedom. I feel quite certain that for the future our conversations will be more colorful more dramatic with life—feeling that I have run the gauntlet of many experiences and their resulting emotions. But I place in your hands the*

*difficult task of reconciling your own years of patient waiting to my*
*bewildering accumulation of scenes and events. We have lived thus far*
*dependent upon each other. I detach from this hour my sense of the pres-*
*ent and I review as from a height the entire plot of the story. From the*
*moment I left you, I love you the more in knowing that you have had*
*the courage to mingle your life with mine. This is dead earnest! Because*
*I look at the whole of it quite proudly, I am tired, Rene. What I should*
*like to write I do not have the energy—you will wait for my return and*
*trust that I will tell you all and everything—only I am afraid there is*
*not enough of time in this life for me to tell you how I need your near-*
*ness. If I were to live forever, time would run out before I could express*
*in the many ways my devotion. I do not need to think of you to realize*
*the loss; it's been there of itself, a melancholy emptiness a feeling of*
*obscure sorrow, sometimes an intense wild anguish—this unconsciously;*
*but then to bear the pressure of actual thought on that vacant pain—I*
*cannot place in simple words the contours of that emotion. You are my*
*light—you must understand. Divine from your music, from the mosaic*
*of beautiful colors and variations, I am there, as I feel for you I want to*
*come home and for us. I want to stop time, for I know being with you is*
*all of time I ever want. If I achieve nothing but the happiness of feeling*
*your nearness all my days, I shall have achieved all.*

*The little photo you recently sent me—smiling through the garden,*
*at me, your hair has grown, it is waiting for me. I dream you from its*
*crown to the little white toes. Mm I had better refrain from this beating*
*my head against the impossible—such thoughts.*

*All I ask is a tall ship.*
*and a star to steal her by*
*And then—on wings of song*
*I will take thee to romance.*

*I have the strangest premonition, perhaps based on desire that soon,*
*sooner than you dare to expect I might return. I can hear your laughter*
*ringing in the fields.*

*And when the moon is full and pale—my thoughts are buoyant as the mist, and I see the warm shadows playing on that dear face.*

*Goodnite*
*I'm tired and the pen is wandering.*


*November 4, 1944*

*[Rene,]*
*I can't think of anything that would better lend warmth to the chill of gray winter days than to receive letters from you, and for myself what better occupation than to forget the cold by responding similarly? I would not dream of having you picture yourself in the field, but for the sake of a make-shift apology to whatever dreariness of spirit I ingest in our future correspondence—bear with me. I shall however do my best for I know these same winter months cast their colorless tones across your life. And so eternity, regardless of you or I remains frozen. Let us prove our heritage of summer and spring and of buoyant life—let us search for the dead leaves buried beneath the crest of ice and snow, remember them as they were.*

*I shall from this date forth number my letters, placing in a circle on top of the first page this may simplify matters—I urge you to do the same. There are favors I also request, each more or less a key to certain humors or moods I wish to retain for the future. Perhaps we can collect the hours of our separation and mingle them.*
*The winter is long as you know, and we must face these next months; you're tired, you've waited too long; there seems to be only emptiness, only despair. But what that you are tired—tomorrow must surely come and the present will only seem as a dream.*

*Darling, believe that tomorrow will come and your fondest longings become reality. My journey brings me closer to you—every hour till swiftly, swiftly I shall come.*

*There is more room to save hope now than the previous months—five of them are in back of us. One by one they will fall back, like obstacles stormed and destroyed—the sweetest moments only I want to remember, sweet only because of the idea that you are there. These days rarely can I hold calm, undisturbed contemplation, but when I do I promise to devote that hour to you. The brink has been, and perhaps remains too close—I cannot afford to squander my living moment. I must find in it,'tho only illusory, the breath of eternity—of things lasting because they are sheer beauty, sheer peace. Nothing exists outside this sphere but the stink of death. And with knowledge only to confirm, but with the pure feeling always there that I think of you as you think of me. This has always been, hasn't it? Yes, we cannot deny it. I love you sincerely as a sister—I want only the chance to love you as the wildness of my heart dictates. These two years have taught me that there can never be any reason to think for me without your being close. Please believe this.*

*When you write, think that soon I will be back and together we can help us forget the bad times. I think I have been here long enough. I'm tired now and I should come home. I'm only human and I'm tired. Why should I go on and on chances become only slimmer....*

*Goodnite*
*Dushenka*

*It seems I've written innumerable letters and they all wind up in ashes. It's been this way for the past months, writing, writing, and then burning. The hours devoted to you lie black and crisp in the mud and you never know. What with trying to untangle and reconcile our old feud and with escaping although morbidly in letters and with attempting to smile or jest, what a colossal piece of futile effort. The argument of necessity has become one-sided, subjective, and awkward.*
*To be brutally frank I see no reason to continue—only by the saving*

*Grace of an undiminished memory can I hold to the effort. I have developed in full strength the constant thought that I am only biding time and if I return, I will still be biding time.*

*Swallowed in the remote lost world was a dream. Since it is gone, the reality appeared, and it dictates what I feel, think, or write. The feeling has outlived months, and so I cannot claim it to be tentative or dependent upon this existence. That once great desire to return home has left—oh not what you think! Only that, wanting something for so long and never having it, one finally ceases to want with any painful degree. I do not reflect your own feelings here, I think, and so we succumb to the basically weak and frail substance of our beings.*

*I can distinctly point out two phases each contributing to the change I have become. One was my stay in England, almost two years; the other finds its date on Invasion hour. The changes undergone to produce a soldier where before was a civilian—there are definite changes undergone: physical ones, mental, and spiritual (by spiritual I mean the force which generates any and all refinement of feeling). There will be one more change, one more phase yet to come: the hour when I know that I am free. This to me is a fantastic thing, bringing such anticipatory delight that I doubt it possible to occur. The past, tho' not unremembered, is replaced by the melancholy tides of quiet, vacant reflection. In the allotted hour of sleep, a familiar tho' vague spirit troubles me with a sweet anguish. He pleads his eternal song and with sad weeping eyes, tells me, "You must not forget us." I allow this "misty intrusion" to steal the moments of peace, tho' I know afterwards the cruel pangs of a swimming nausea—the lift and sink which finally envelope oblivion.*

*I wait, nothing more. I do not live, I only wait! Wait for the day when the walls crumble and the fresh strong sunlight bruises my body and soul. Or a darker night absorbs the consciousness of me.*
*You see, I have nothing to say, nothing to write about, and this letter I will mail for the sake of letting you know that I do try to write. What*

*do you expect me to do? To I can't write anymore, I can't! I'm only a number on a dog tag—only dogs have prosperous lives.*

*Men are wounded, sent to hospitals, and return to frontline duty before they are well. The supply lines are long, too long—it is hard. The winter is settling in; men live on the ground in water-filled holes. Men live like rats and die worse than rats—they lay still in the mud and blood, and their folks wait to hear from them not knowing, not knowing.*

*At home people are complaining they don't make enough money, they strike. Do they know what it means to have one day and night without fear of being blown to bits, or of lying in a ditch with a bullet cracked skull? Do they know what it means to have the comforts of a white bed, of a bathtub, of clean clothes, of being left in peace and quiet, of going to a movie and laughing, of having someone close to you, telling you "I love you," of feeling a warm body close to you? Do they know what it means? What is expected of us? Two years of misery. What is left of us here since D-Day. Who has ordered this and why do we obey? We are forgotten. Why weren't the heroes sent home instead of pushed forward month in, month out?*

*November 4, 1944*

*My Dearest,*

*I wait impatiently for word from you. Since leaving England the silence has been broken only sporadically, and now the meager, little letter will not do. I must have many! Could you possibly fail to see this? If you have thought to be near me, how best to do this than by writing constantly? For myself I should be relieved and happy to answer any questions that have tormented you. Yes I know the bitter misunderstandings and dissonances have made you loathe to write. Perhaps you*

*This undated self-portrait is signed "Me."*

*think that I am again appearing as one who takes things for granted, and that I turn hot or cold at will. I am willing to wait. Putting the question directly, I expect no vague answer. Do you wish me to return to you, or are you progressing in the thought of wanting to forget me? You know how I feel. I want to come home and have one chance to prove myself to you.*

*If you say you must forget—you had better prepare ample reason and still I'm afraid reason would never satisfy me. So perhaps you had better make up your mind to have me for better or for worse. Ha sounds like a proposal. I have been seriously thinking of marriage—but if I can't have you, I'll do very nicely without it. I know definitely when I return all scores will be evened....*

*November 5, 1944*

*[Rene]*
*I think I can safely say that you and I have entangled ourselves in an extremely complicated mess. Follow me as closely as possible, Rene, because what appears to be a hopeless situation must be adjusted and ironed out. And we are not going to be deceived either by fortune or ourselves. Let's get at the root of all this damn trouble. I'm responsible for it, and you have done wonders in enlarging it.*

*In the beginning I got involved. My last letter explains it in more detail. Well I did you grave harm more psychological than anything else. Dirty, stupid fool trick I will never forgive myself for. I had no idea it would never die out. There were the days before I left we argued out this problem, but I had already implanted that distrust in you. So now, no matter what I say, or prove be deed or action, honestly I do not expect you to favor me. But I will keep trying to regain your love. Believe me, dearest, I have not broken that trust of body or heart.*

*There is nothing lost on my part, and I live with an eye to the future. I'm a little "beat up"—one hour with you and I'll be fit. I only need a little love, a little confidence, and most the reassurance that I have not hurt you beyond repair. You have the unenviable problem of coping with doubt I understand the logical premise which first you will make—that I being a man could never possibly live two years without betraying at least the trust in the flesh. My closest companion here is one who is married and has pursued the strictest continence. I cannot say for the rest, except that perhaps they were wisest since their mission promised only death, and for many it has proved itself.*

*From experiences in both cases; it is erroneous to believe that soldiers are immoral and loose. On the contrary, civilians rolling in the lap of comfort, luxury, and time prove to be insistent sensualists. This Casa-nova business is more appropriate to the civilian. At least the soldier is frank; he demands the body and not the heart while the civilian demands the body by reducing the heart. Hardships while draining the body of its energy also produce a neutralizing agent in the limbs. Of course you do consider other pressures, which drive any psycho-logical traces of desire into a semi-existence. This simple preaching, however, does not make me a saint as you once imagined. Although if I've said it once I said it many times; you must have faith in me.... Sometimes I wonder if all is not just another demand in my own mind.*

*I'm tired—I hardly know if I present any convincing argument, maybe some of the sentences are worded roughly—when I want so much to be kind and quiet. Yes, there is so much that is confusing. Everything is suspended in air, and we pluck indiscriminately at the thoughts—many times leaving out their counterparts. I'm tired and not sure if I have the right even to think.*

*November 14, 1944*

*Dear Mom,*
*Received your nice letter of Nov.14. I'm glad to know that you are*
*receiving mail without too much waiting. I hope you don't mind if I*
*write to Dick without making special efforts to write to everyone else. I*
*should hope the letters are meant for everyone concerned.*

*I received a few days ago a package from Walter containing a sweater*
*and three good books. I think it was a nice gift—greatly appreciated.*
*We are coming along as best we can under the circumstances—feeling*
*fine and fit. And I sincerely hope that you, Dad, and everyone at home*
*keep up your already long wait in the best of health.*
*Perhaps you don't know that I realize how great a strain it is for you*
*— but I'm afraid it can't be helped.*

*Give Ann my special thoughts and is Papa still working at the cellar?*
*Well, good night and I'll be seeing you soon—that's what I've been*
*saying for months. Ha! Maybe it will happen.*

*Love to all*
*Affectionately,*
*Ugo*

*Thanksgiving*
*November 23, 1944*

*My Darling,*
*I had almost forgotten—today in America is Thanksgiving. I had*
*almost forgotten that I told you to meet me at the flowerbed.*
*My thoughts were far from this—very far. It is difficult or impossible to*
*detach myself from this breathing here. Even mentally, I write this by*
*force, only as one who follows an ancient path accustomed to its famil-*
*iar route not by sight but by a deep rooted sense.*

*I know how futile effort is to translate feeling in words. If it were possible I should hesitate to do so—it is futile and meaningless and empty. There is nothing here. I am nothing—I live with you, and perhaps I'll be no closer than what I ever was and what I am now to you.*

*I keep searching for the line that suggests horizon, but for more than two years I've searched in vain. All is illusion, this reality; for it is exaggerated, violent, grotesque, incredible, confused, aimless; it probes too deeply the shadows; it unites death by living with it and stalks destruction. The soul pays the price of the crime the body and mind perpetuate. The particles of love are shattered and die daily. The world loves with its mouth, with its oratory, but it practices destruction with a keener insight it understands it. As long as it puts its faith and hope in the future of another life it will know nothing but oblivion in the illusion of both worlds. They are only names we created, illusion reality. They try to give order where there is chaos of thought. Looking for excuses or reasons for our actions, our destinies. It is all burdensome. To the civilian death is only a word with a vague meaning—it is rarely spoken of—to him it means a sure Kingdom of clouds and singing angels—the average person believes that he is eligible for this region—somehow he will get there! So does it matter how unscrupulous he lives here? He can always find time to pray at the last gasp. Our minds cannot grasp the idea of Heaven and Hell—it represents an ultimate retribution or reward; the eternal. By every indication manifested in nature and all living things, Heaven remains locked in the human brain, and the rest of deception, ages thick encrust the keyhole and Hell? I have found it. I wait only for the thread, which holds the sword to snap!! I will be free from the idea of Heaven or Hell.*

*November 26, 1944*

*Dear Mother and Dad,*
*It's me again. I hope you are both well and manage everything all right.*
*I am fine and looking forward to the day when all this will end. I just*
*wrote Harold another letter in answer to one I received. I'm afraid we*
*are still too far apart to see each other. He is in one sector and I am in*
*another.*

*We manage to keep warm enough and it is not too cold anyway. So*
*don't worry yourself. When I was in Holland I met the nicest family.*
*Remind me to send them something when I come back. Because they*
*took me in. Well—I'll tell you all about it when I return. They are the*
*cleanest people in the world.*

*I didn't realize how homesick I was until I actually sat down to supper*
*with them. Their son is a blacksmith and I watched him shoeing horses.*
*It's quite an art. They had a Victrola, and we brought some records*
*there and had a good wholesome evening.*

*I guess I'll be disappointing everyone again this year—but maybe—for*
*sure, I should be home next Christmas. Leave a place on the table for*
*me anyway, and Harold too. I'll be expecting your Xmas mail soon, and*
*I wish to respond with heartiest wishes and the best of Christmas cheer.*
*Maybe the Huns will call it quits by then. Give my love to all and to all*
*goodnite.*

*Affectionately,*
*Ugo*

*Chapter Seven*

# DECEMBER 1944:
# THE BATTLE OF THE BULGE

## HOLDING POSITIONS

Broadcast in AEF Radio Weekly on Sunday 24th December 1944 at 10: 30 and 2230 BST
UNIT SPOTLIGHT: 29th UNITED STATES INFANTRY DIVISION
—Edward V. Roberts, United Press Correspondent

It has been a long haul from Omaha Beach to the banks of the Roer River, inside Germany: the 29th has never stopped.

There has never been enough written or said about this frontline American outfit, and the part it has played in the assault upon Hitler fortress Europe. Since D-Day, security has clouded some of its proudest accomplishments: how the men with the little blue and gray shoulder patches stormed ashore in the face of one of the strongest German concentrations in the beachhead area; how they took Saint Lo, where their wounded filled one orchard and overflowed into the next; and what they did at Perrier, and at Brest, where they held the right flank under direct fire of a battery of huge naval guns.

With Brest cleaned up, the 29th struck northward, across France, Belgium and Holland ... and pounded its way into Germany, smashing a corridor through the concrete and steel of the Siegfried Line.

Since June, the fighting men of this Division have expended more than seven million rounds of small arms ammunition alone ... a bullet fired at a German for every 35 seconds that have ticked off since H-Hour on D-Day. They have cleared mines from more than twelve hundred miles of road, which ultimately leads to Berlin. The Division has captured more than its own number in German prisoners. The total of casualties it has suffered must still remain secret, but the 29th's Roll of Honor is a long one.

Beyond the Siegfried Line, the Let's Go Division paused to regroup and rest, and incidentally, to win the somewhat dubious distinction of being the first American Unit to conduct maneuvers inside Germany. This came after the capture of the German town of Wehr. Wehr was thoroughly and effectively captured, and its German Defenders were ousted in short order. But the job was not done entirely to the liking of Major General Charles Gerhardt, the Division Commander. (The General is something of a perfectionist.)

So two days later, the few German civilians who had sifted back into their homes were evacuated once again, and the 29th proceeded to go thorough the motions of capturing the battered hamlet once again … this time to the General's complete satisfaction.

Gerhardt is one of the American Army's most capable assault generals. He was short and bald, and peppery and profane. Significantly, June 6—D-Day—was his birthday and he marked the occasion by storming ashore with his men. Three hours later, he was bawling out officers of his staff for failing to be in proper uniform.

Headquarters of the 29th always is close enough to the front lines to hear the chatter of machine gun fire. The walls of the Command tent are spotted with patches covering German bullet and shell holes. Each patch bears a neat inscription as to the date and number of casualties.

When the 29th was ready to jump off on its last push, the General summoned his staff for a last-minute conference. When they were assembled, he marched to the war map on the wall. He punched a stubby forefinger at the Roer River. "We've got to get the hell on down there," he said. "Let's go."

That's all there was to it. Ten days later, the muddy, bloody men of his division crouched in their new foxhole along the river. To the rear word was sent in this sector, there is no more German opposition west of the Roer. The 29th had done it again.

The great obstacle to be overcome by the 29ers was the series of seven massive dams, which sat in the Hurtgen Forest and held the Roer River in absolute control. One hundred million tons of water could be released to make the Roer a racing flood, which would overflow the approaches to the River along the fronts of the First and Ninth Armies. (29 *Let's Go*)

There would be no further action until these dams were captured. This was not to occur for quite some time, as on December 16, Hitler launched a massive counteroffensive, known as the "Battle of the Bulge." Field Marshall von Rundstedt employed three German armies, consisting of fourteen infantry and ten panzer and panzer grenadier divisions in this operation. They struck in the sector of the Eifel Mountains on the First Army front in Belgium. The main impact of the blow was delivered on a 75-mile stretch of line, which was held by only four American Divisions, the 106th, 4th and 28th Infantry Divisions, and the 9th Armored Division. The aim of the counteroffensive was to break through this weakly held sector, drive to the Meuse River and ultimately continue to the great port of Antwerp. The north sector of this drive was approximately thirty miles south of Julich, and posed no threat to the 29th Division. (*29 Let's Go*)

The 29th Division assumed control of the XIX corps sector which had been committed to reinforce the beleaguered forces battling in the Bulge. (*The Long Line of Splendor*) During the remainder of the month of December, the 116th Infantry continued to carry out its mission of defending and improving positions by setting up interlocking bands of fire, clearing fields of fire, and taking all preventive measures possible to guard against the Germans counterattacking from the East bank of the Roer River and penetrating from the North. (After Action Report) There were 151 casualties during this phase.

*In the past few days I have not been familiar with myself,—a sense of growing uneasiness estranges me from a previous attitude of tolerance and last night's sleep was wildly haunted—they are not frightening images strangely enough—but they come with terror in their eyes. One face caught in a whirlpool of darkness swam up to my own face and the eyes held such terror!*

*It is difficult to sleep, and there is no rest from fatigue. The mind keeps going while the body brings sleep.*

*[December 1944]*

*My Dearest,*
*I suppose we all act thermometer-like regarding the war. I am not the exception. In view of this I can do nothing but tell you that it may be long yet, however, the day will come, and I hope that time rushes fiercely. What can I say—since you know my attitude? I do not hope for anything but the war's cessation, for me to return. Time does not move*

*as rapidly as before. I'm afraid we shall hardly know each other—and I have so much to tell you.*

*There are many letters of the past in which I have reflected morbid hours—please forgive me this. Loneliness and anguish are strange dictators. I refrain from writing, since when I look soberly at what I have written, I close my eyes and try to picture your formula for living and I behold that I cannot mail you pages soaked in the rancid brine of my own tears; I should detest myself! Tho' I am not concerned with philosophies for living, since the overwhelming madness of this existence does not permit of such ideals, I still consider that I must bring home to you a heart that is not encrusted with scars. Within, I remain the same; when I cease to respond to this madness with grief, then you shall know I have deteriorated into something not worth your infinite waiting.*

*Sleep is infested almost nightly by images of a familiar memory, yet I cannot begin to tell you that they torment me with a new distortion. I live again in sleep, the hours of the day, only with great, fearful distortion. At this time, what is most appropriate to write about? Since I see and feel things as being tragic to the extant of ridicule; Yes, I wish to hell I had been born with the idiots' bliss, so that I would not feel out of place in this nonsensical version of being. I do not find myself responding savagely with the savage. Men die or are killed—it is pure knowledge, clear as sunlight, that all things must go why do I respond with notes of pain, of sensitivity of shock? How stupid! Why does this simple, plain, ancient custom of killing and being killed torture me by first straining itself through my imagination till it becomes monstrous, gruesome, mad, utterly mad? At this time, and for that matter, at any time what is there to write about since the fire must come to ashes?*

*How utterly ridiculous my boast of eternal love since a conspiracy, destiny, has placed my mortal body and mind (there is no other) in a perilous position. And how stupid it is for anyone to mourn over pages illuminated with passages of violent ethereal emotion. Oh yes, it is quite dangerous to think this way, but oh my darling, I only want to come home and love you before we grow old and before it is too late. Don't you see? I know how empty, how cruel disillusionment invades the childhood faith. The only truth is the knowing that truth is a word people have sought to create meaning for.*

*If I were braver, if I were stronger, I would not be alarmed to tell you that you wait at your own peril, but I can only suggest this, since the only life conceivable for me is to feel your love about me. And I confess, if ever you grew tired and bade me farewell, I confess, I would go quickly mad. True, I have lived long without you but I am not sure now that I am sane. Of Human Bondage has a strangely beautiful note, but I must not write of something, which I reserve only for sanity. I made another note here for a projected conversation. Don't pay too much particular to what I say since I almost persist in leaving out the counterpart and I hang things in mid-air. I'll cut them down when I return. I have said nothing, only words, words empty, futile, hopeless, powerless. I am here and you are there. See? How insignificant and ant-like we are. Minds that voyage from planet to suns with bodies insufferably mortal. It is too real, too personal to reveal on paper how I need you to understand. There isn't much to talk of tho' I've filled the pages.*
*I would like pictures of you. Would you oblige? Winter is here to stay it seems making things more grotesque. I fail to see any meaning to all this myself. The thing which gives me a great lift is to read how encouraging your armchair prophets are. They actually make the wonderful predictions that the European War will end in a few years. Isn't that just dandy? Of course we are glad to give all; especially when prolonged over a period of years. After all didn't the boys who died in the last war do so in order that we would have peace? They didn't die in vain, they died for their country.*
*I'm not so bright, just tired, that's all.*

*I look forward to returning—there are things to do and people to avoid. A new world? Ha! The same old globe wearing a different face.*

*Sketch of a fallen soldier.*

*Hello Little Angel,*

*That character steps out again from the places you read about.*

*Well, those places are little schools; the educational system cannot be questioned. I think I mentioned before, that if Christ lived again in this world he would be crucified all over again. In fact, Christ dies daily. And another one is born only to die. Caiphas still lives, so does Caesar and Pilate. Every year the manger cradles Jesus and every year Judas sells him for silver—30 pieces of silver, or 30 million dollars. The plot remains unchanged; the characters wear different clothing, and there are tall skyscrapers in the background instead of Oriental mansions.*

*"The Passion" is a play of life everyman is destined to play a certain character unfortunately but then again; there is nothing fortunate in the idea of life. Schopenhauer, as I recall, pointed out the truth—also he noted that the truth is far from being pleasant. That was not his fault; he only shoveled some of the obscuring mind of deceit from it. Every decade or so, a new prophet impresses his way into the Palestine of our lives— we fall before him, when our heads are bowed he decapitates them. For twenty-five years I've watched this, the most terrible sensation of all is that I was born with this suspicion—only I wanted to see for myself. I saw, now that suspicion is pure knowledge, and I am ashamed that I doubted my earliest impression. I am ashamed that I had lacked faith in what I believe.*

*The story is there, written by the hand of time, by men who wished to paint the picture of it so you and I could make a civilization without floundering in the trap. But our egos—(I'll leave out mine) take the whole story personally—instead of profiting by its great revelation. We spend our time bowing before its human representations of good and evil. I'll stand by, and my arm is there in spite of yourself. I shall grasp your passing form as it willfully flounders towards that heritage of darkness. I am ashamed that I hesitated and was confused only because millions rushed headlong into darkness and I looked longingly towards the light, I almost betrayed those few great lights but, tho' I am caught in the whirlwind, I battle furiously in the opposite current. There is one more beach—I'll make it! Meanwhile the light burns with, what appears to eyes long accustomed to darkness, a strange intensity. It may be that Autumn grows more beautiful, more splendid with color as it turns ashen and dies, or it may be that Spring smells sweetest before Summer's heavy fragrance drugs the senses into an incredulous joy.*

*December 1, 1944*

*Dear Mother and Dad,*
*I received your letter of Oct 25 today with the pressed flowers enclosed. The colors are slightly faded, but the shape and old spice fragrance brings me to memories, and especially now as the Christmas season nears there are so many happy scenes I recall. It all seems so distant and more dream than reality. But I'm sure someday it will be reality. I haven't as yet received any of your packages, but I expect to shortly. I received a letter and Christmas card from Harold yesterday. He is back in Luxembourg. I hope he stays there.*

*You make my mouth water when you mention all the stuff you put up for preserves. I'm glad you got your winter coal in. Got to have heat you know!*

*I knew it! Too much worrying is giving you and Pop weird dreams. You had better get some sleep at night. Ha! Well before I close this short note, remember to keep your spirits up and keep hoping. Merry Christmas to all and to all a thousand kisses.*

*Affectionately,*
*Ugo*

*December 6, 1944*

*Dearest,*

*Are you receiving my mail? Yours has not come in almost two months—
it seems ages indeed! Please remember to drop me a line as soon as
possible. It's bad enough not having you near; without the added
burden of not knowing about you.*

*Can't you see that you must talk to me? Unburden your spirit, for I am
waiting. I request you to think that, at the present rate our correspondence would cease utterly in another year. We are not like that are we?
We would not betray the glory of the past at a time like this. Don't you
see? I am accustomed to this strange way of living, and perhaps these
habits will not leave me. This is all right; at least I appreciate the idea
of hope. Everyday I say to myself every step forward is a step closer to
Rene, and I almost love the ground that falls behind me. Yes I've spoken
your name many times. I know you didn't hear; how could it be? But
the ground was going to pieces all around, and the sky kept falling in
white hot layers, and all the time I kept thinking that I wonder if she
knows that now there is only a split second of eternity between us, and
I used that second to call you. I remember still, my body trembling and
my hands buried in my eyes when that first wave of terror passed. I lay
still and smiled, when I had no business smiling because inside I kept
waiting for the earth to split again and I thought, God she can't hear
me calling above that noise and what's the sense anyway of bothering
her? I can't be sure of meeting her now or tomorrow or at anytime. I
shouldn't scold her for not writing—maybe it's best she forget....*

*December 13, 1944*

*Dear Mom,*

*Was happy to receive your Christmas package. Boy it was delicious!
I'm saving some for a rainy day—or rather, for a sunny day. Seriously,*

*everything was intact. The cheese on the surface was a bit mildewed, but inside it was O.K. The cakes were fresh as if newly baked. Come to think of it, I've been missing a lot of good meals. You're as good a cook as ever, and I think with delighted anticipation the pleasures of being home and chewing on some of that stuff. The boys here had such large eyes—I had to forfeit some of those biscuits. But I had enough to satiate my bird-like appetite. I was gaining weight in England, but I dropped a few pounds in each country, I think.*

*I hope you and Dad and everyone are in the best of health as I am. Evelyn wrote and said she was sending me gloves, nice to look forward to. How is everything back there? Do you get any information on my outfit? It's been on the secret list since I left America. Ha!*

*Next package you send enclose magazines and anything else to read. The winter is long and lonely. I'll close this short note thinking of you always and hoping you keep hearing from Harold.*

*Love to all and*
*Best Cheer*
*Ugo*

*December 16, 1944*

*My Dearest,*
*Hello. I've been reading where a quota of men from the Western Front is being sent home on furlough and for reasons of recuperation. Although the majority of these cases never saw more than six months overseas duty, and in some cases much less, they are being sent home. These men have been wounded one or more times and also carry two or more decorations. It would cost me that much to come home and then I should leave again. I have nothing more to say you understand.*

*Well it appears as tho' all the pessimists who manufactured prophecies of a long and furious war hold the favored ace of hearts. I am quite used to these disappointments since you realize soldiers live on rumors. They usually result in rose-colored lenses. My spectacles have the glass knocked out from such furious scrutiny. So once more I must remind you that the waiting can be doubled, tho' it has been despairingly long. Perhaps in the long run it will have a happy providential twist. I don't know.*

*You see? I'm only one where there are millions. It is the unpleasant truth. Writing, by necessity of circumstance, is forced into a confined channel and I'm sick to death of it. The enduring cry, heard above every day and nights existence is that when, when will the hours pass? This hour which has paralyzed all of a man's reason on earth. Of the future I have never spoken of since there is no future until the present hour dies. And when it does—I will laugh.*

*Pull your belt one more notch around your heart, and when you think there are no more notches please let me know. What do you expect me to say? Rather than give you the impression that you are waiting let's remember that we both are waiting, for the same thing—true I am also waiting for freedom. It is quite different. We will save the subject.*

*December 20, 1944*

*My Dearest,*
*Your letter of Dec. 2 arrived today. How good it is to hear from you in such clear, warm accents! But how sad I am to know that our mail disregards its own importance, its own urgency and arrives much belated. I do not wish to envision the 66 days you have lived through without receiving my messages, however, know this; every hour of existence voices to the universe, my silent incommunicable love—that same universe holds you, surely you must know. Do not consider the possibilities of trying situations to alter this fact. I love you as before, if not*

*more, and I shall love you when I return with the profound memory of this hour gone from you. It is difficult for me to think—to write!*

*There have been recent moments which left their impression on me, and I have been shakened by the roots. My nature, long repressed, is not dead, and the blows fall two-fold. Now the struggle with myself is not kind. Having come thus far, I entertain fatalistic tendencies. It is not my blame, I was born what I am, and I must destroy what I am to keep a normal mental attitude. You will understand. I trust to you for tomorrow. There! I wish you would cease urging me out of myself.*

*That enclosed clipping. It must be terrible not knowing. Well I am not that image. I am far from there. But I believe your last conjecture was the true one. Cameramen are allergic to my outfit—besides I'm hiding behind a not "too kept" pair of handlebars.*

*Capturing Prisoners, Alsdorf, Germany.*

*December 22, 1944*

*Dear Mom,*
*Received a package from Rodelli and two more from you. Everything*
*intact—I enjoyed the chocolate and cheese and all the good things.*
*Thanks again, and send my thanks to Michael also. I am in the best*
*health and hoping you are too. By the time you receive this the holiday*
*will be over and then maybe one of these months the war may be over.*
*Who knows?*

*Tell Walter I received his note of Dec. 2, also received a Christmas card*
*from Dick and Evelyn. I hope you had a nice time on Christmas Eve. I*
*guess my Christmas will be spent as usual. Everything is quite the same*
*here, anyway. I guess maybe this world is still the same old world—as*
*crazy as the weather. I don't imagine I will return until this ugly busi-*
*ness is finished here. Too bad the people who hold conferences couldn't*
*be here—they might act a little differently.*

*All in all it's a pretty sorry mess to live and be ruled by pathological*
*people. For surely I am not wrong.*
*Well I'll close this short note.*

*Goodnite and love always,*
*Ugo*

*Chapter Eight*

---

# JANUARY 1945:
# CROSSING THE ROER RIVER

---

## THE LONG WINTER

In January, the weather was bitter cold. The men dug in and tried to stay warm. There were active small arms battles, a firefight in Julich, and continuous patrolling of the River. Old men of the Division wounded in Normandy and Brittany came back from the hospitals in January... they came back strangers, looking around blankly at the new faces in their "old outfit" (*29 Let's Go*) The policy of General Eisenhower was to return men to battle, as many as three times, after being wounded. Many times these men were returned to different outfits, and this was a great morale problem. Both sides played the propaganda game, and sent over leaflets:

In *29 Let's Go*, J. Ewing the author, quotes one of the German leaflets: "Who is going to launch out into the new battle? Statesmen, Politicians, Big Bankers, Munitions Manufacturers? No, NOT ONE! Just you the men of the 8th, 29th, 102nd and 104th Divisions, average young Americans with your lives ahead...." During the battle of the Bulge the leaflets read: "Or do you still think you could break through our lines and advance to Cologne? You came as far as the Roer River in three costly offensives. Now it is our turn! Our armored columns have broken through your lines on a sixty-odd mile front in the Eifel and have penetrated deeply in Belgium. Your future is dark. What are your hopes? Surrounded and fighting to the last, wounds and death await you. We can give you at least one last hope. This senseless hopeless battle—give it up!" On the American side, our propaganda leaflets enticed the

Germans with menus of food fed to POWs. The Germans had lists of officers: 1st Lt. Maier (3rd Co. 69th Inf. Regt. "You are indeed a shining example to your men. It is one of your principles never to be seen up forward. Your favorite expression is, I'll shoot the hell out of you!"

*January 1945*

*I am lonely and uncertain; that you know I travel in loneliness, feeling my origin unhappily differs from others. They are blissful; they are happy. The past is not dead; I feel still the scorch of its flame within; the brine of its tears still burns, and new sorrows replenish the deepening streams. The past is what I am now, and I assume its ever changing forms, its old poverty, its old glory. My childhood tenanted an enchanted castle on a secret isle, and I ate abundantly of its rare sweetmeats, and my soul breathed in the perfumed opiate it offered my senses. I was lord and master there, and I ordained the happiness I found not in physical being.*

*My home was a vast pretense; my laughter rang empty on my ears. My eyes beheld untold miseries, and each time I reached to touch them, I saw mud and the chains on my hands. And the world's battering ram crushed me with its poverty, its sickness, its ignorance, its blindness, its insanity, but with closed eyes and pain filling that darkness, I still saw my secret island with the great cliffs frowning at the sea and that great house massive with treasure.*

*I listened with open eyes and stunned soul—my mother and father while they destroyed my house. And so early, quite early I left with my brothers to be alone. I returned one day from school and the house was empty of furnishings, quite empty. My mother was weeping, and my father was gone. I left school quite early to share the poverty. I got used to the cold there—that solid winter with frozen feet cutting trees, and I learned the use of the spade. I have not forgotten the hundred pennies in a dollar. Nor the hurt pride to receive the charity of food and fuel—for I was a Prince! Tho' I knew well how far my island lay, and daily it was gathering its indistinct outlines, and the sound of sea crashing against its shores echoed with diminishing faintness. The city caught me in its vulgar sounds and I spun with the wheel of progress and someone bound me to its flaying spokes and smashed me in the mud and blood of strange shores.*

*Progress hurtled its hell of sound and fury through cathedral and town, and left the dust of cities choking and blinding me. Religion caught the terrified soldiers and pounded their prayers into the pulp of mud and blood and ignorance and earth. I rolled with progress over the stains of what were my comrades. My soul lay impaled in the wheel of progress, and it was liberating and smashing and burning and rolling and reaping a thousand graves. Progress rolled thunderously forward, and the sharp steel of the rod cut into my flesh, and soon I knew, it would cut the steel from my wrists and I would be taking the road back. They are sleeping quietly with snow, pink snow covering the graves; and they feel no pain. But my wrists wear white grooves, visible only to them.*

*January 1, 1945*

*My Dearest,*

*I know you have not been receiving mail from me lately. But I have written many letters all of which I condemned as inappropriate to send. So my letters may neglect you, but I have not forgotten. There is no such thing as memory nor such hope as the future, without your image gracing both.*

*The temptation is strong to write how I feel, yet I succeed in banishing the grotesque beauty of the past. And when I am done with a letter, I am relieved to think I need not send it. Of the present, I prefer to avoid discussing of our relationship—you and I are aware of its attitudes. There is indeed much to talk of but a tempest does not permit our voices to be heard above its fury.*

*You would do well to write I make the awful blunder of forgetting that I do not mail most letters. I write and so by return mail I expect answers to questions you never receive. I live more than ever in a strange world of my own fancy, and there are things too intimate, too illusory to write about. I have no other alternative! It does not become easier, this being away. The months and days grow longer in the time of my mind. I cannot grow used to this, as I cannot accustom myself to the idea that I cannot see you at will.*

*Many times I am grateful to you, for being there. To whom would I lean to if you were not there? Thanks for your Xmas pckg. It will last me quite a time: I wish I could share it with you.*

*Damn! Rene it is my turn to confess that I am not the better for being gone so long. I am ill with a desperate desire to return. It obsesses me completely so that I cannot think, or feel anything but rage. I've got my own ideas on what life is and I find that I am betraying my own convictions. In that respect only my conscience throbs. But it can only happen once unless I am a complete fool! Only a handful of people, people we never knew, have caused this war. I propose most determined resolutions; if only I could come home. I would never leave again on my life. I love you. I haven't said how I love you. That's what you want to hear. If you understand that I do, then you will not mind my other thoughts. When will it be over? Night falls on the just and the unjust, and we have no power to direct it. I am tired, restless, utterly fed up with all! I shall never be the same and I am happy in this thought because I am free, tho' I am bound. I will talk to you someday, and your spirit will be freed because I think it is mine. Form your own conclusions on this, think what you like, but I am free from the snares. For I cannot reconcile myself to the idea of a God who would permit such infinite sufferings on his beasts! Surely I did not will it?*

*Goodnite, Love*

*Night Patrol, 29th Infantry Division.*

*January 4, 1945*

*My Dearest,*

*I'm writing this note, if for no other reason than to alleviate one day's disappointment. You can indicate on your calendar that on this day, I remembered you: Darling if I can't write every day you can be more than sure, I think of you hourly.*

*My job is to be with you as much as possible in as many ways as I can imagine. And if you suspend an entire evening's program—just to rush home and read a note well, you could be forgetting for awhile, but if you insist on poring over these miserly messages I can't do less than write. I should have asked you before will you send me a few copies of magazines every month? And anything you think I would enjoy reading. You discriminate. I sent a German Helmet home, have you seen it yet? Mom wrote and said it impresses her too much! Would you care for a skull? A ray, a hank of hair, a bone? Or perhaps a bottle of odor—not perfumes, but stink! I have all these and more at quite a reasonable price. Ha! Ha! What a guy! I will remind you again to send me something to read. I hope you are still purchasing what records and books you can. Pile 'em up! I hope you don't mind if you note that I have written this at various scattered days. The date doesn't mean a thing.*

*Goodnite and keep well*
*Love always*

*January 7, 1945*

*My Dearest,*

*Your message of Dec. 15–25 arrived today. I do not know where to begin an answer to these notes. The letter is crowded with mental and physical distress in proportion to the unhappy sufferings you endure. And it is so since a loving heart cannot be insensitive to the Hell the mind can conjure. I hate myself for this hour that I write because, where before, I might have read your messages with wild pain now I look stupidly and vacantly at your utterances of grief and longing. The pressure of these many months has benumbed my senses; the knowledge that I am helpless to comfort you in your distress, or to come to your side now and before when you turn ill. To be crushed out of feeling the old sweet sadness, to be made a stranger to the idea of love, of life, of hope. It's a filthy rotten deceit the inhuman tempo has made me to think of myself and myself only—but only as an animal viewing constantly his instinct to live. Everything else is dream, illusory, fantastic. My life with you comes only as a haunting consciousness in spirit, another world. My writing is a great effort to appease this memory and I do not trust it to be real. I can think of you now only as a period of time detached from the past. I experience the unhealthy faculty of thinking upon you in the light of that lost life, that you were ill then, and that you suffered untold misery I can believe and feel the punishment of response but now, there is little I can say that would not cast off a reflection of this existence here. Surely you can't urge me to respond in a normal way. And for this you must understand and forgive because when the nightmare wears off the opiate will vanish with it. Until that time it is best you remember me as the guy who loves you and will return to love you with more understanding more reality and less dreams. How can I comfort you now? There is no way except for me to be home—the time for words is spending itself almost vainly. I feel damn silly even writing. I want to get home. You are ill, my mom is ill—what is the use of writing, of talking about it? Somebody started a big fire and we have to fight till it's out or we're out. This is the price we pay for ideologies, the garrulous chatter of demagogues, of old senile politicians. That's why we're killing and being killed to satisfy the smug vanities of men who want fame and glory, to revenge the hurt dignities of international names. To settle their private disputes by sacrificing young blood, young souls. National vendetta! I want to come home. My only quarrel with man is his shallow pride, his god damn conscience, his eager belief in another man's words his inclination to prostrate himself at the feet of the first character who says, "Let's fight for" and then a lot of empty, meaningless, high sounding ideals. I was not born with the idea of accepting any body's idea of truth and standing by it til death—because to me there is no truth absolutely none except personal desire.*

*The wills of people bend like frail stalks knowing not their own power until it is too late. It is not reasonable to believe that there is anything sane behind the bloodshed or after all this talk of post-war condition the development in economics, science, the great strides in aeronautics, living conditions, housing, utilities, the great strides in medicine, the organizing of groups, more and more groups for training, for communities, for etc., etc. For this then is war created? For the movie industry to commercialize on it. For authors and men to write books, to exploit a man going through Hell and standing by, watching the final agony—so he can write about it and fill his pockets with 30 pieces of silver. Everyone is partially to blame for this. They teach facts in school rather than wisdom. Institutions for the betterment of greed; art, noble art is trampled in the grime.*

*I don't want symbols or representations of freedom. I want Freedom of mind, body, and soul. And it cannot be found where the coils of civilization wrap around you. Why all the talk about Freedom, ideals, religion, from stinking orators who know nothing about it except what was told them? Take all the newspapers with their human exploitation and filthy, rotten propaganda and burn them! I am here where I can see the full final shame of all this talk. This slow agony in mud is the result. The reliving of the "Passion" daily, the exhumation of martyrs. History rolls by thunderously, and I am caught in its spokes when all my life I looked at it aloof, separate from a lofty height, now I struggle with the rest yet somehow I am still gazing at it as from an impersonal height. And it gives me a peculiar strength, a confidence that does not shake with every turning of the wheel. And now you see I am unchanged. I have not given an inch from what you remember me to be....*

*January 14, 1945*

*Dear Walt!*
*Received your letter of Dec. 27. I thought it was nice of you to try and carry Christmas through. Regardless, I am well and hope you and Jo are also. Will you look out for Rene? I know she is not well. Maybe you can write and give me the details on this since I realize she has refrained from doing so to avoid causing me undue concern.*

*I'm glad to hear you are still plugging; your day will come but you make it to find it. I hope to be home this year perhaps. If it's O.K. with God! Ha! Ha! There isn't much to talk of I'm afraid. I still expect news of Harold—haven't heard from him in quite a while. However I expect things to be what they will. Say how about purchasing a bottle now and then of some scotch, etc. etc. It keeps one looking forward to warmer and merrier days. I have cultivated a slight thirst. Ahem! Nothing noticeable of course. Well I'll be back soon to laugh over tragic anecdotes and weep over humorous ones. I'm anxious to return to see what it is we were fighting for. (I think I know.) And when I return I'll tell you the secret of providence if it is good to me.*

*Thinking of you during this prolonged vacation.*

*January 17, 1945*

*Dear Walt,*
*Received your letter of Jan. 9. I hope long before this note arrives, you will have heard from Harold. The point is that some of the mail may have been sidetracked due to the current offensives, since I haven't heard from him either.*

*Whatever the case may be, it is absolutely pointless and in fact harmful to worry—anxiety in itself while quite natural is more often augmented if it becomes a morbid habit. Let's try to take things a bit more lightly since our very lives and reason to existence is, in the broad view, ridiculous. And what we put such store by in our futile existence is inevitably shattered by the indifferent universe.*

*Life is there, so we cling to it, human parasites, and we make much noise in so doing actually it is nothing to lose. In times of crises, if we can look at it from nature's ruthless attitude, and in its true perspective, namely that of insignificance, I think it is easier to bear. We must avoid our humanity to partake of the inhumanity of nature. This may be dangerous in so far as social convenience goes but it is expedient to mortal pain.*

*The knowledge that you at home will be able to bear sanely whatever news—is a source of relief and courage for me. Be kind. We have many miles to cover before this is over.*

*Araneo is in my own division strange that you should be the first to inform me that he was wounded. I am quite up to date with the current news in U.S. I imagine you will be working in a defense plant soon. That's fine! I say this because I wish I were working in one instead of this—Don't let it be too late.*
*Rene writes but not too frequently. I'm afraid she has been ill for a long time. If only I could get home! I feel that I have no more business claiming her to wait for me. I've been gone so long and I may be gone long yet. And what if she waits in vain? You will take care of her for me.*

*Thank Joann for the books she sent. Really I have all I want—no need to send packages. These things have become of little necessity. Thanks for your thoughts anyway.*
*Send my warmest affection to Mom and Pop. And tell them to be good.*

*Affectionately,*
*Ugo*

*P.S. Write a bit more often if you can.*
*P.S. Again tell Mamma and Papa that I just finished their last Xmas pckg.*

*Alsdorf, Germany, 1945.*

*January 22, 1944*

*Dear Mom,*

*I was greatly surprised yesterday to catch a glimpse of a most familiar face riding past in a jeep. The face echoed the same note of surprise. He jumped out of the jeep and ran forward with outstretched hand. I shook it roughly and happily, and the first words I remember saying were "you cause a big commotion inside of me but I can't place you. For God's sake who are you?" He called me by name and it worked out that he was Eugene Serino—remember Harold's pal? He hadn't changed a bit and I hadn't seen him for years. I only knew him slightly, but I felt like he was an old and welcome friend.*

*He came overseas four months ago. I dragged him into my suite of rooms, a stately German Hotel with a stove, a radio, and boasting an excellent example of American artillery (the walls caved in). He looked around and said, "You don't do bad, do you?" All in all, he envied my winter hospice.*

*But it was good to see him! We talked over some things and he told me he used to visit you. I'm glad! I gave him Harold's address also. He talked very highly of Ann, and I told him I regretted not being able to make her acquaintance a bit longer; before I left.*

*If you have any time, drop over to his home and tell his folks about it. Mr. Frank Serino, 194 Shepard Ave. Being very appreciative, I showed him a few battle sketches I had roughly made. I will write to Harold about this incident. Eugene tells me, Harold is a hard egg when it comes to letter writing I believe it! Ha! Ha!*
*P.S. I did mention that Harold was quite lucky I didn't meet Ann before he did. I wonder why women attract me? My intentions are not particularly scrupulous, I might delicately add.*

*Well? How's "the Voice" these days and her adoring Patron Pop? Young as ever? Good! No sense getting old—it's not quite the fashion these days. I will write to Evelyn in another letter, meanwhile thank her for her two packages—gloves are fine, but peanuts get seasick en route. A few more months of winter and soon the sun will shine maybe brighter and warmer than ever before on this sad, crazy earth. Meanwhile, all my love to you and all the kids.*

*Affectionately,*
*Ugo*

*P.S. I'm hard headed and I still love Rene, so it's wisest if you two accept the fact without the usual female nonsense.*
*P.S. Look Mom, I think she is ill; be a good nurse will you? Thanks....*

*January 25, 1945*

*My writing—past letters inclusive—hangs in midair, surrounded by nebulous unreality. My writing then, expresses nothing beyond pure passion, pure feelings; intellectual only in the gray pallor of its own instinctive morbidity. It is vague, because who can describe what feeling is?*

*I have moments—incommunicable transports of the wildest journeys of the imagination. And when I return to the sordid gray of reality I am uncertain which is which, and then it is. I know how vast and brilliant is that other life which knows no language, no civilization, which enjoys the fulfillment of all desires. How we do talk! As if our actions did more but reflect the real desires. I have none of you, and you know not the secret of my arms. We have taken for granted the legacy of art—it is never understood. You have your beliefs, I have none; you have your illusions, I have but one, which is you. This I cling to with a silent acquiescence, a sense or feeling of need for ultimate survival. It is dangerous then for me to feel that you are a separate being holding separate ideas—this then is the strange, selfish, violent sentiment with which I seek to engulf you in an overwhelming love. For I know I am alone and you are the hand closest. It is fortunate for me I met you, and perhaps unfortunate for you. I cannot picture the normal life with its petty undertakings, its habits, its pleasures—I cannot accept its principals, its aims. I am a fever almost of impatience for the moment to end all moments. This then is my mind: Can you unravel this problem? You must! I will be a good pupil, but not a serious one.*

*January 31, 1945*

*I've been thinking about the past. The home, the folks, the way I lived. The practical and impractical existence. The situation now, with three brothers married and me left holding the so-called "bag." Things will be different because I am changed. When I look back at poverty it appalls me! The memory of early privations, early dissensions, dispossessed houses, debts, depressions, hand to mouth existence. I was never built to cope with grim reality—my life, to attain its cherished hopes, had to be dream, but that dream is shattered. Art is the leisure of wealth, and I have no wealth, but wealth I will have. And I mean to get it, in proportion to realize these desires. I cannot possibly live, as before, I cannot! I must think that someday there will be an even fiercer holocaust—I want refuge, security.*

*Chapter Nine*

# FEBRUARY 1945:
# JULICH FINALLY TAKEN

## IMAGINING SPRING

There were two major factors holding the 29th Division in a defensive position at the Roer River. The first was the "Battle of the Bulge." Hitler's offensive began on December 16, 1944, which was to be a battle of immense proportion. The United States had 600,000 men in active combat; with 81,000 casualties including 15,000 captured and 19,000 killed. The Germans had 500,000 men, with 120,000 casualties and dead.(*Going Places With The 29th*)

The crossing of the Roer River was the second factor that held the 29th on the West Bank of the river. General Eisenhower's orders were to begin three massive thrusts toward the Rhine River. The Ninth Army and the 29th Division were to come from the northeast. (*The Long Line of Splendor*) The impending attack was designated "Operation Grenade." The Ninth Army and the 29th Division were to clear "all German forces from the area west of the Rhine, in order to seize the Rhine River crossings north of the industrial Ruhr."(*29 Let's Go*) The attack was scheduled to begin on February 10, 1945, but the Germans, before losing the last Roer dam, were able to inflict partial damage to one of the floodgates in such a manner that a less rushing but longer lasting flood was created. The Roer overflowed its banks; the current was dangerous and fast(*29 Let's Go*), and the attack was postponed. A new D-Day had to be scheduled, and the men had time to build up tension as they practiced river crossings. The 29th Division was divided into three regiments—the 115th,

175th and 116th—and each regiment was divided into three battalions. Sometimes one battalion would be assigned to an altogether different regiment as in Phase 111, where the third battalion of the 116th was attached to the 175th Regiment.

"The 29th had been sitting at the gates of Julich for three months. In that time the city had taken on a character tinged with mystery and foreboding."(*29 Let's Go*) Julich was an ancient city named by the Roman soldiers for the Emperor, Julius Caesar.

On February 23, 1945, the Ninth Army's push began across the Roer to Julich. The commanders of the 29th were promised the heaviest artillery support of the entire war. At 2:45 a.m. the guns of the 29th, reinforced by those of the XIX Corps and of the 83rd Division, began an unholy roar; in forty-five minutes they pounded more than ten thousand shells into German positions across the River.

*February 3, 1945*

*My Own,*

*I have received your letter of Jan 3 in answer to mine of Dec 10. I forgot to number them. It's no use—I keep forgetting the previous no.—so we will discard this system. However, I wrote quite a few letters and I hope you receive them all in reasonable time. You must not mind. If I forget the contents of mail I write previous to my latest letter. I don't mean to appear unstable, or confusing or contradictory. It is difficult for me to set in order my constant thinking of you. It is so vast, so overwhelming the place you tenant in my life; I cannot hope to define except during the miracle of calmer hours.*

*I have been fortunate to be able to say that I can still write you. My gratitude to the powers that be is immeasurable.*
*The emotions are physical when I write to you—my whole body trembles and how violent an ordeal you cannot know. Dear, sweet Rene, I am living to return to you. But I cannot write feeling this way, perhaps tomorrow, tomorrow.*

*Know this: there is no rest from thoughts of you waiting and I know I must return! I am able to pick up now after a few hours lapse, the continuation of this letter.*

*Your letter comes not unaccompanied with tenderness and completely I allow the gentleness of those sentiments to soothe over the bruise. I was born with this need and you were made to administer that overflow of love. I remember you with great kindness and you have not failed that memory. In your waiting—you have renounced all, the best of your years, for me. There will never be enough I can do for you but I feel I have done nothing. I shall not rest until I have given you the best of what I am capable of.*

*I have carried you to England, France, and now you are here with me, inside me and if you are a burden to me then I press its pain deeper into my soul. It is all I know of life, and I cling to its nebulous softness and breathe deep of its fragrant nearness. There is nothing in any letter I would tell you, nothing I have ever said in this eternity of separation that contains meaning above or beyond my simple need of you, body and soul. In my hand tonight is the cool one of yours. And I crush back the reality again and again the tenderness of this dream.*

*I reread over and over your letter—it is all I have! All I have of you, my heart will burst with longing (how inadequate the words are) I love you little angel. I hope and believe you are feeling better than usual—this has been a greater strain upon you, who wait in anguish and uncertainty, my own hours are at least spaced to recognize certain times of trial and certain periods of comparative safety. Besides I'm quite used to it and there doesn't seem to be any exterior result to inner agitation.*
*I might have imagined I wrote you before, in thanking you for your Christmas gift. In case I didn't write I'll thank you now, "Thanks darling."*

*I've figured out when I would be coming home under the rotation plan—in about seventeen years! Ha! One must have several decorations and one Purple Heart with cluster attached. Of course politics plays a lead. I only hope that I might be able to come home before entering any Pacific campaign. I'm only a number and those armchair strategists feel no qualms of conscience in playing checkers. I do expect home front action to prevent any such procedure.*

*In any event, we will not anticipate too much concern over what is not probable. But it is an uncomfortable thought and it comes often enough! When we are finished here I expect to be one of the comparatively early arrivals home. If not, I'm afraid I will have nothing more to say. But here's hoping for the best—things usually see me through—at least up to the present writing.*

*Give my special remembrance to your folks and the kids.*
*P.S. Unfortunately my hair is too short to comply with your sweet request—believe me. But here's one kiss to herald the thousands to come. One embrace; a prophecy of tomorrow's spring and home.*
*Love always,*
*Ugo*

*February 4, 1945*

*Your mention in your letter of Jan. 3, wondering, by my abstract speech if I possessed other loves, other faces, other influences of which I had kept secret from you; no there is no mystery but the inner one, no face beloved in that childhood but yours. You have been the one human upon which all my emotional needs as well as the physical ones have been well met.*

*That childhood was consumed not listlessly—it is not so far a past dream but I recall it as being a time lived in the absorption of its every vital moment. Our first years together remains as significant and as fresh as the last ones are now. They were immaculate as the first breath of passion must be. I shall never forget the thousand secret treasures of those young years. If I did not shout my exultation then I strove silently to embrace to its depths, to preserve what would be fleeting. They live forever, the happy treasures and you the greater part of them, and because of you they are rare lusters that shine even in the gray or the dark.*

*There is something, a secret which has been mine for many years of which I will tell you now and of which I will never again make mention of. I must communicate, through some means of expression, some creation, to you and to those kind people who travel a life consistent to the simple poetry of simple truths, communicate my response, which alone the joy of which overflows and becomes lost.*

*I've had every thought of writing to you this night and because I felt too deeply, too violently the passions of this relentless depression, I have avoided so doing, but I am drawn irresistibly to the solace of even your memory; how helpless I am in its presence, and how with wild abandonment I fling my soul at your feet. The daily conjured image of you is familiar, even more so than the real you, to my most despairing longing. It has heard my every tenderness uttered even tho' it be through closed lips. And so I write of what I dare not; violating your sweet faith and shaking it by my own unendurable weakness in the face of this endless trial. Rene, I'm tired of this consistent, unchanging, inexorable existence. I urge the weeks, the months forward, forward! but the new ones are the old ones and time continues in its own circle. We age but time remains frozen to its immutable orbit. To be separated from you is horrible, but to find in that separation also the double hell of being here. What manner of world is this? Surely it is mad! A vast asylum where frenzied minds prowl and stalk destruction to be destroyed. But they are clever, using special keys to lock the heavy chains one cannot move.*

*The sound of men expanding their ideas through violence; the hysterical dissonance of religion screaming its prayers through centuries; the furious thumping of a tribunal's hammer passing judgment and condemning the already condemned soul; the hollow soul-eating threat of exorcism from society if one does not accept the seeds of a dead generation, whose lingering pestilence of fear born thought, living beyond its projections, multiplies only to strangle the next generation. The sibilant, slithering tentacles of dead men's ideas and ideologies winding their coils about and crushing with a slow pressure the freeborn spirit of man. The melodramatic demagoguery whose vague kaleidoscope of eloquence asserts some bursting egoist and the unreasonable thud of peoples prostrating themselves to the ground at its feet. The eager clamor as it lifts the dictator, this creator of vulgar noises to the highest pinnacle of idolatry. The forced march of mind and body through the mechanisms of civilization; the melancholy, leaden monotony of search for hope beyond this life; the gray procession of monkish images with furrowed brows and cadaverous cheeks, denying the instincts of flesh and sense to feel in life its death and by this, imagining they touch the real life.*

*The Lorelei blast of bugle, which plunges the young blood of nations into some fantastic dream of blood and valor and romance. Is the victory won? When the victor lies a stinking carcass, ugly, broken, yellow and clotted with dust and blood the sound of glory is empty.*
*The nervous irregular pulse of crowds, crowding itself from the earth. The scraping jangle of slaves' chains as they try to move their spirits fettered to the ancient rock of a decayed philosophy. The self-conscious wild-eyed disheveled oratory of anarchy shouting from its outcast height. I am become identical to the universe; my activities are those of observing and loving a child's tears and feeling that child's suffering to the extent of absorbing it completely—loving that pain out of existence.*

*My prayer to find a language that I might communicate to the beloved the immortality of love—love as the "I"—not the outer I who contends with Dark Tides of civilization, but the "I" who gazes at a raindrop on a bough or leaf and finds a tender joy in the simple beholding of it, in the knowing that it is beautiful because it is there.*

*It cannot win! I am mated to the green grass and the hurt wing of the bird; the sun is in me and the darkness will go! Shatter like a black mirror and sky open up before me I will fall into its blue bright lure. Soon my friends will say is it him? Then we never knew him and we cannot hope to now!*

*My love will frighten you, but I believe you will find that fear to be only a vague ignorance, a doubt. Soon it will vanish and your eyes will smile again, brighter than before.*

*When suffering and loneliness become incommunicable where are the words to use? And where is the heart that will listen? Is it not all a dull painful confusion? The world is of children who, incapable of reaching compromise over a question, seek decision in War and destruction.*

*February 14, 1945*

*Dear Mom (Mme. Butterfly),*

*I received your sweet letter of Jan. 29 today. Your expressions and sentiments left me deeply moved; though I would you had happier feelings, I am drawn irresistibly into that gulf of sorrow, and I share it with you. If we find relief in so talking of that loneliness then it is best we talk of it. I confess now that Harold's silence strikes an anxious note in me, but it will do no good to suffer a premeditated grief. Until you receive definite news, and when this occurs, it will be either good, in between, or bad news. There's only one type of bad news and that you have learned long ago how best to accept it. The other in between news is not so cruel as you imagine it might be—one hopes and one does not lose faith in waiting. I know you are a good soldier and remember I am always with you and when the going gets a bit tough—just lean against me, will you?*

*How did you know I was there at the dinner table Christmas? And don't you hear me raising hell through the house during the day and night? Be a good and careful girl and when I come back we will both get a little wine where it does most good. O.K.? Hal Ha!*

*I'm glad you heard from your brother—don't worry, things are not as bad as newspapers paint them up to be. In fact very few people in this world really starve. (I haven't seen any and where haven't I been?)*

*I'll keep that address you sent of my cousin—who knows I might be able to locate him.*

*I had forty-eight hours in Bruxelles, Belgium, recently. It was my first leave in many months. I had a damn good time—knocked myself out in cabarets and hotels. I was sailing high most of the time. Ha! Ha! I had a particularly good time at Maxine's where I met a dancer named Mimi (as in La Boheme.) We spoke French. She danced and changed costumes twice (for me). The next day she came an hour before I left and took me walking through various shops. I think she was a good girl; I didn't have time to find out in detail. She was quite lovely and walking with me I felt suddenly very rich. She was romantic enough to purchase me a little souvenir which in return I offered a kiss.*

*Now I'm back in Germany and she is dancing at Maxine's in Belgium. I'm a bad boy! Ha! Do I bore you?*

*Send my regards to Ann and say that I miss her also. Give all my love to Eve & Dick and of course to the younger generation. And how is the (Drawing)?*

*Tell him to keep the moths from digging in defenses in my coat pockets.*

*Goodnite*

*Love always, Ugo*

*P.S. Keep my love life locked with discretion or fifty women will commit suicide.*

*February 15, 1945*

*Dear Walt,*

*Your most encouraging letter of Feb. 4, arrived today. I say encouraging because the sentiments you expressed concerning home and the news that you intend to return to East Orange are nice to my ears. I am happy when I think that every one home is happy. Yes, I know Harold has not written, but we must allow ourselves generous time. News will come; whatever its nature, let us not overdramatize our feelings. We were born to accept the knowledge of life and death, and we will not cringe before its inevitability.*

*I am keeping well and warm, and these months of winter are almost gone. Let us hope the coming months bring the sun and peace. Perhaps I should not say this since the Army dissuades hope from a man. The greatest disease on this earth is the military disease. I have studied soldiers closely, and the ones who like this existence are mentally, morally, and spiritually deranged. And if one lives in close association with those afflicted, one becomes also incapacitated to feel or think. We are the prisoners of the bigwigs, but you at home control them. Generals pursue their careers at the expense of suckers like myself! I regret not having held the courage of my convictions. But it would have meant prison either way. I am not a fool and perhaps I am dangerous because of it. There is no peace in the thought of another life after this one, so I cling tenaciously to this illusion of one. The price of living within the circle of civilization is too great. The price is always freedom and ultimately death, or suicide. One must be an unknown, a phantom, anonymity, or one must have power to live—one must crush or be crushed, this is God's earth.*

*I do not hope to return home without first satisfying the ambitions of war lords who cast nostalgic eyes towards the "setting sun." When the country is in need its manhood is called, but when its manhood is in need, to whom can it call, or turn to for help? Be not surprised and remember when a man seeks his freedom he seeks it desperately, and he will find it! I am not a robot! Tho' for three years, or three eternities, I have worn its armor. It is becoming heavier on my tired soul, and it must breathe! Soon!*

*Play for me! Play for me so that l can breathe! When I return I shall go to an asylum to find rest and sanity amidst the neurotics. Ha! Ha!*

*Very well. Here's a gag, I'm having a swell time and I enjoy not seeing
the prospect of returning. If only there was the remotest date, I could
count the days, the hours! I think you had better keep this letter under
your belt. After all isn't the truth always hidden? And you know it is
difficult for me to write other than what I believe is truth. There is no
end! Why does Rene wait? Because I tell her to? I love her, but she is
only a ghost to love another ghost.*

*Please write soon.*

*Goodnight*

*Affectionately, brother,*

*Ugo*

*February 22, 1945*

*My Dearest,*

*Thought I imagined what smelled of Spring (purely imagination I
assure you) or maybe memory me walking. The last traces of winter
underfoot, on the street and houses; the sudden street lamps, come
to life. I breathe deeply a warm current (like Spring hope or premonitions of wild fragrances). I hurry to meet them (wherever you are they
become manifest). I behold the house with its conventional awkward-
ness (I have loved it for the hours, years I spent there). The dying sun
dies (the world prepares for evenings rest or tomorrow's struggle). But
I am free, freer than the birds who have never been caged, and tonight
I pause (just outside; one foot resting on the stone step). This is her
house, and here she waits. Spring pierces me now and I know I have
arrived. "No she has not returned from work yet." Where can she be? I
wait in the parlor, lighting a cigarette, and Winter, the unforgettable
winter of war engulfs me, assaults me and crushes me to its bosom
of ice and loneliness and fear. (My hands tremble at the temples and
I stare off the shattering recollections.) A light step patters its way
through a horrible booming, a sweet singing voice, a white winged*

*thing circles above a battlefield, a vision of Spring shapes itself from the image of a desolate village, from the frame of wood and glass—you appear, you speak or sing. "You here? When did you come? Have you waited long?" No answer, only bright eyes meeting mine and then the answer, articulate with the muscular energy of arms, hands, body, and lips. Spring plays its delirium of soft, sweet smelling things about me—its caressing grasses cover me; its dews cool me of fever, draining my soul of ache. In its embrace I crush the grasses between my fingers (apple blossoms stain whitely the grass), and my fingers grasp and sink into their petals (till they bleed white sticky juices). "Yes, I have waited in this torture of waiting all day, for you. But you are come and I am come and the pain of the hour is gone, eternity is here, let us remain here." Rene—do you understand? I'm a mirror reflecting what I feel you must feel. Say that it is so.*

*Write to me—anything—only write, please. It means so much. I know it's difficult now and increasingly so—but it would help—so much more than words can say.*

*Love always,*
*Your own Ugo*

*February 23, 1945*

*Darling,*
*I am asking you to marry me. Which means I expect an immediate answer. I cannot tell you of plans until I know if you will accept. You see, I've been thinking of all the things to do, but I feel uncertain unless I know your answer. I allow so many dreams to come—and they are such happy dreams of the future—they are of us two, together. It will be fun meeting the obstacles and surmounting them. Let me know of what you think. (Please say yes.)*

*February 24, 1945*

*Dearest,*

*A word about the mail, which arrives at a furious pace—approx. one
letter a week. How can people be so damned unimaginative!
I seem to thrive on loneliness, it's always included in the menu. This
must be a nightmare.*

*What happened to everybody—are they really nothing but memories?
Nothing has been an able substitute since I left—to fill the infinite gap
at my side. The months are becoming years, years!!! And I kept telling
myself long ago that tomorrow, tomorrow I'll be on my way. And here
months later I'm still here, as if all this time never really happened;
so I'll talk to myself and think the same things over and again and
again—yesterday, today, tomorrow!*

*February 25, 1945*

*Rene,*

*Your letter of Jan. 8 arrived today—today I wish now I had not lived
to see this letter. You will read about this day and the momentous ones
previous and after this day. The news will tell you where I am, how I
live, but not why I live. As long as I live and have breath I will tell you
"I am destined to die loving you." I am of the dirt now—it covers me
with its scales—and I too, I myself live it, with the soil. I am before you
(as you willed it, on my knees begging you to understand) and to think.
I will give you time to think—no not to think, but to feel me! But your
answer will not come to lift me from my waiting agony.
"You are aching to say goodbye to me." You have said goodbye—it is
done—I will say it when I die—you shall never hear it.
I had forgotten, for a while the plaster casts. Do not send them home.
Destroy them with the letters. I request you not to leave to anyone those
things (which are me).*

*You are free of me, completely, irrevocably, forever. I have lost you—but you belong to me—you are mine with every breath my soul takes—and with every breath, a greater pain brings me nearer—nearer to peace.*
*Goodnite, Goodnite*
*Ugo*

*February 25, 1945*

*I'm going to tell you what you will never forget for the remainder of your days. You have punctured and drowned to its final end the total of your love, of your faith and of your inner spirit—in this; a letter only today arrived, dated Jan. 8–9.*

*Beside me, is the first letter I wrote in answer to this perverse letter, only today received. Only today! I read it through and with each reading of it the gray reality of what you are grew more distinct. Again I reread to seek a desperate negation of the impressions you had created—but I read in vain, the reality stared, stark and deliberate, and my heart (which you have crushed) rose out of its drippings of grief and froze into an anger such as, if I were there then and—even now; I swear, I should strike you fully across the face—and allowing the release of long pent ambitions, proceed to discover those frail semblances of men—who have lodged their filth and narrow souls between me—and what I have ever loved. The "bourgeois" lovers who have proposed to you—since I went away (and am I to believe without first engaging you in the preliminary preludes of sex?)? If I return, I return too late I will be sober with suffering but if I were there now. Where would your "bourgeois" be? Is there not enough of blood on my hands that I could not then find true justification in the seeking of more personal blood?*

*It is too late to retract the venom you have spilled upon me. I am Ill with the oppression of nine months' battle. I am ill with shock and shattered nerves. The memory of escapes, the sounds and smells, the sights, the too often remembered eternities of Hell. Even now, I would tell you nothing, even now when it does no longer concern you. Where I am, under what conditions I write. You don't know, nor ever will. I must go now, and tomorrow I will write if I return.*

*I am back but to what? Why? When there is no beginning, no end to what I should do, say or think. I am in a hole—writing by candlelight— or the sky shattering into intermittent light—or perhaps in the chill cellar of a ghost town. I have done well (so I thought) not writing to hurt you, telling you of love when all about is death. But it is too late now. Mark the day well—it has been great news for you people. Great news.*

*Before I continue—let me suggest that I mean to write without thought of composition, or order. Just read and let it sink in.*
*Do you wish me to quote you? No just search yourself—you will remember what you have written to me. You are selfish! Narrow-souled, a pretence to womanhood who is incapable of loving. You are sensitive— yes, to feeling pain but not sensitive to simplicity, nor beauty of spirit, nor avowed love.*

*Chapter Ten*

---

# MARCH 1945: MÜNCHEN-GLADBACH

---

## WHERE TO NOW?

Ugo wrote his own After Action Report for March. The town of München-Gladbach was the largest German city captured, with a civilian population of about 20,000. "It was a silent and curious, but unhostile crowd, in marked contrast to the civilian temper in earlier towns in Germany." For the first time since D-Day the 29th Division was relieved of frontline duty, with the 83rd Division to their left and the 2nd Armored Division to their right converging. "The 29th was out of it... we're through fighting... we're staying here!" (*29 Let's Go*)

The After Action Report illustrates the forward push into Germany. The roads were wide open, and the number of men and amount of matériel were astonishing. As the Defeated German Army began to retreat, one man commented, "This is how a rich country fights a war."

*München-Gladbach-Rheydt*
*Germany*
*March 2, 1945*

*29th Infantry Division M.P. set up traffic control station in center of Rheydt*
*Town badly battered by aerial bombardment and artillery. Mar. 25,*

*The unstoppable flow of men and materials.*

*streets now cleared of rubble by Engrs. Approx. 12 ml. back of front
line. The first time since D-Day I have been as far back as Army & Corps
areas. First respite since D-Day from frontline activity. Hear at night
only the intermittent roar of 105 guns. Last night, Lufftwaffe operated
from visible distance we drenched the sky with ack-ack, and red tracers.
Heavy military traffic thunders day and night through town.*

*Prior to Rhine offensive we rotted away in an agony of boredom
and loneliness in Alsdorf. Terrific artillery barrage prelude our spear-
head across the Roer River on the dawn of Feb. 23. Escorted prisoners
from Aldenhoven to Div.P.W. First two days. Crossed Roar R. into Julich
on pontoon bridge. Julich completely leveled, smoking ruins, the gray
color of battle shrouds the scene. Roads bad, muddy, town with bomb
craters and artillery shells. Welldorf, Merch, Munitz, Guerlsdorf, Titz,
Holzwieler, Immerath, Borchenich, Keyenberg, Wauls, Hockneukirch,
Juchen, Wickrathberg, Wichrath, Gresenkerchen, Rheydt, Munchen
Gladback*

*Very little sleep—too busy transporting prisoners from front to
P.W.E. Where to now?*


*March 3, 1945*

*Dear Mother,*
*Just dropping you a few lines because I know you might be worried
about us. I am feeling fine and especially now when I feel we are driv-
ing the last lap of this crazy race.*
*As I told you before many times, let me do the worrying, I'm in a better
position to do so then you are.*
*I hope you have heard from Harold because I haven't yet. What's going
on back there? And how is everyone?*
*Well here it is March already. I understand you people had some
unusually severe weather. I think I've become weather conscious out
here—besides a few other things. I don't think you will like me anymore;*

*I'm incorrigible and drunk with the fever of war. Even tho' we smash
everything in our way, the civilians appear to be relieved, now that we've
come—they were expecting us I suppose as they expect the inevitable.
Things are a bit confused and we're handling a lot of Poles, Russian,
and Italian workers. They're happy as larks—they say we're liberators
—I tried to speak Italian to some, but I get confused and find I'm
speaking French instead. I must have been gone longer than I think.
Sometimes I suddenly realize what miserable, destitute, homeless,
purposeless creatures live on this old earth.*

*I've seen things and been places, which are the naked world and I don't
think a good bath, a nice bed or some soft music will make me forget
the truth behind the surface.*
*Well send my remembrances to any that remember me.*
*And I'll be seeing you*
*Soon (?)*

*Goodnite and sleep well*
*Most affectionately,*
*Ugo*

*March 13, 1945*

*Dear Mother,*
*Received your nice letter of Feb. 26, today. I am glad you received
those two statuettes and whatever I may have sent you. And you asked
if I received all your Xmas gifts. Yes. They all arrived quite some time
ago. Thank you. I hope that when this letter arrives you will have
heard of Harold. I have heard nothing from him and have no way of
finding out. We are in two different armies. I hope for your sake and
Dad's that all is all right. You did right in having Dick inquire of his
CO and his Chaplain.*

*Some news should be forthcoming soon. Inform me immediately of whatever you hear concerning him. I am glad that you and Dad are well and keeping a lot of courage—we always need that. But even more so, we need the will to live in the face of hard, inexorable life. I miss you dear—it's been such a long, weary time—it staggers me to think of all that has happened—during this terrible period of separation. We've all been fighting a personal war besides this more brutal conflict.*

*I am not at all happy to know of your censorial attitude towards Rene. But since you wish to do well and pass this sad news for my welfare— then I am grateful. You see—dear—when I left Rene was a rare creature—if she has changed my heart has changed too.*

*Please do not write of her again—never, never again! I want to forget this bitter strife. I won't ever fall in love again. I want nothing, absolutely nothing, but to come home and be left alone—in peace. If someone dares mention anything of Rene when I return—I swear! To kill them. I do not intend to see her again or anyone, and this bit of news need not travel beyond your own knowledge.*

*I have had enough of people and the world—you would be surprised how insignificant and harmless they are when dead. I want nothing of women except the satisfaction of being able to hurt them—I have been hurt enough! I am going to prove difficult when I return—but I will do my best to avoid dissension—but I want nothing in my way. The people who have hurt me will live to regret it deeply. I have seen enough of shallowness, of greed, of selfishness, of hypocrisy, of deceit—I will be left alone. I look at the world with all its peoples and I say they have brought this great crime on their shoulders—let them suffer the price of their ignorance. I am no longer a child —I never remembered being one unfortunately. My sympathy for others extends to the length that I have been hurt—and it surprises me to see much misery without a pang of feeling. Yes, I am difficult.*

*They preached Peace—and then they preached War—the heart is consistent to only one of these, but it must suffer the two. I am ashamed to live in this world—but I will not hesitate to call the hypocrisy by name nor the ignorant—and those who profess love must first live love. I am sorry to hear of your relatives—but it's the same world. I guess all the good news on the Western Front has you guessing when the war will be over. Well the war won't be over for me until I can wear blue trousers again. Besides, I'm only a number in the Army that gets pushed all over the world. But when I leave Europe I'm coming home on my own if necessary. I have no desire to see the Setting Sun. If I'm fighting for Freedom—Let's sample a bit before it's too late. Well, I'm tired of writing—it don't mean a thing anyway.*

*Goodnite and keep well*

*See you soon*

*Affectionately,*

*Ugo*


*March 13, 1945*

*Dear Mother,*

*At first I thought of sending you a cable but after inquiring I learned that the swiftest mail is a letter. Harold has written me a short letter dated March 3. He is O.K.! This information should reach you within ten days. And I guess it is your Easter present Mother, to know that he is well. Apparently, he was in a hospital at the time of the Belgian offensive— because he doesn't mention anything about it. He had a cyst removed from his heel. But he is well now. I gather from his message that he does not write often because he claims he has difficulty writing. (Please remember this for the future.)*

*I think I understand he complains of the war never ending. Ha! Ha! The months are piling up on him. I better write him and explain that one does*

*Road check STOP ME.*

*not grow accustomed to loneliness and being away. I guess we will sort of weep on each other's shoulders via letters. He is no longer attached to the Third Army. It is easier for him to locate me however since the division has become quite a legendary name. Jerry at least gets nervous and quits when we're around. Of course he throws the ball hard. We are better known as "The Destruction Company." Ask Hitler how the guys who were killed on Omaha beach came back to haunt the defenders of Brest and ST.LO. Ask him who is responsible for the Normandy break-through, ask him, who the ghosts were that crushed the SIEGFRIED line. Ask him, who spearheaded the present offensive. No wonder I'm tired! Ha! Well, this time I bring happy news anyway. Harold is O.K. and I guess that's all you want to hear. I suppose Ann will get drunk at the news. Ha! Don't tell me you worried Ann! Women are fickle, besides being absolutely heartless. Why don't you write him a severe letter? He will just love that. P.S. He told me he sent you a bottle of perfume not to be opened until he returns.*

*Goodnite Mother and a pipeful of pleasant memories Pop!*
*Sorry to disappoint you but I have no purple heart yet—what am I saying!!*
*P.S. I'm mailing some packages of art supplies home.*
*Tubes of paint are irresistible.*
*Love to all*
*Ugo*
*[29th Insignia]*

*March 14, 1945*

*Dear Walt!*
*Have received letters from both you and Joann—it seems strange to hear you discourse on musical theories, stranger yet, when you remind me that you are still as enthusiastic as you ever were about certain attempts I made at painting. I regret having left any of them hang-*

*ing on the walls—they are a constant reminder of me and I go about life trying to forget and be forgotten. Dear brother how can I possibly continue writing to you and to anyone else when I feel I can no longer repress from writing the violent depression of both physical and mental natures. You don't understand? Well I will tell you in secret.*

*I am through! I feel I cannot endure much longer. How easy, how simple to sustain physical pain, but this mental torture which decries no horizons end and for which effort at enduring is not rewarded. I have fought off the accumulations of horrible hours for a long time—to me a lifetime—and these hours have been assaulted, besieged by the added burden of collapse of all I have held most dear. What at one time was of the utmost personal is now resolving itself into a common confession of primitive grief. If I have appeared apathetic inwardly the greatest activity always prevailed. Whatever miserable attempts I made of concealing my shameless ability to suffer, by writing empty nonsense, a fake humor, or of covering all with symptoms of courage; I now confess writing will not permit these veneers to exist I must discontinue to write or forever burden you with the dissonance's of my spirit.*

*The tyranny of the world has descended—vulture like upon my soul and is expending its furious appetite upon me. To the very rock chained I have seen my comrades struggle for awhile and ultimately fall limp, lifeless and still chained and from beyond the rock, I listen to the mad hollow laughter of peoples—as coming from a vast amphitheater. Only then, by these frail symbols can I express what is inexpressible. So I am torn by the wildest of passions, the rage, the bitterness, and the silent grief—silent because it is helpless, and I fall—a child half slain, waiting for the escape.*

*Putting faith in you to hold this intimate letter, locking it in your heart, and never breathing a word of it to anyone I continue.*

*For two and one-half years I have lived for, breathed for, dreamed of Rene. I must tell you this or go mad. I have loved her violently—with all the energies of the senses and of the spirit and now, now I wish to extirpate from my every conscious moment, any thought of her. Do not ask me why! Only never again mention her name to me. She can never again be what once she was to me. She is not what in fantasy I dreamed her to be. And when I return she must not be there—or I will hurt her as I have been hurt. I cannot recover from grief—tell me to recover twelve years of life with her—it would be easier.*

*I cannot possibly explain in detail the combination of circumstances which has led to the severance but have felt for a long time that it was the inevitable end of so beautiful yet so painful a love. She also, of this attitude, (perhaps the intuition they speak of in women) has not been discreet in withholding from me this finality of things. I speak of this to you, perhaps to convince myself of it, but not to alleviate the sudden overwhelming flow of hopeless tears. It was cruel of others to write to me when I was so helplessly far away from her in such shameful and unworthy lines. I cannot possibly forgive anyone who has involved her with the pettiness of common scandal. When I left, I left an angel, but I have been gone eternity and other influences, other lives have intervened have changed, have destroyed her faith in me.*

*Can you conceive the love I had for her so strong, being the absorption of me, above and the deep of me, violent to excess, gentle to humility, slave and master, brother and lover—never content to voice its unutterable passion. The sight of, the living with, and the knowledge of death has rooted it deeper and I know (inexorably) within me. So that my very feelings mock my separation—yet I must fly from her. So delicate yet so primitive a passion I have held that this knowledge, of other hands, other arms enfolding her waist, kissing her lips, pouring their dead souls utterances into her ears has all but impaled me with a terrifying mixture of rage, hate, revenge, resignation—and everlastingly of silent sorrow.*

*And this to be carried, added to the inhuman burden of war. Have I escaped death so many times to emerge to suffer this living death? Oh I am alone walking benumbed, dazed amongst the brutal orgies of civilization I have clung to the idealism of her, of her, my last illusion. And what is life without illusions to blind it into feeling and thinking a happiness, which basically does not exist? Lavish misery, abundant melancholy resolve themselves into quite another emotion—and this has no parallel with the metonym of words. So how can I explain myself even to myself? I am ill with all the long repressions of body and soul and the one I loved has become a mockery has indeed mocked with bitter sarcasm's and doubt, these feelings set into being by her, by indeed Rene. I am writing, this vital me, only to find apology for whatever course I choose to best forget, so you who understand best the abnormal sensibilities and reactions of your brother who displayed artistic premonitions once, will not be misled.*

*Painting at best was only an early suggestion of what fires were as yet kindling. How can you know the immense receptivity, the all-absorbing intensity of thought and feeling, which wrack me now? How can you reconcile me to even your own understanding? By a mere memory? And how can she know of this?—When I left her—so unceremoniously, so casually? Perhaps I am to blame—never really speaking the love I had for her when we were together.*

*But since I have extolled it, pronounced it, lent it flame in all my letters— these she regarded only as mere outbursts of a fettered instinct. Beyond this and below this—was a time when I was not so secure—when I despised myself and avoided her saint like questioning eyes. But since—I have not betrayed any trust she had in me. I swear from the moment I left her, she has been my constant thought, my hope of tomorrow—the purity that I have never found was contained in her memory. Why must I talk— when always I will love her, with a bondage that cannot be dislodged but I perish with it. She has told me Good-by—and I have answered her. And now please destroy this letter and never mention a word of it to anyone.*

*Affectionately,*

*Ugo*

*March 15, 1945*

*Dear Walt,*

*Interrupting your letter of Mar 5 with the observation, brought home
very acutely to me, that the preponderance of personal misery blinds
one to the fact that others feel a kindred pain. It differs in degree only
as the individual differs. But we must lift ourselves above ourselves; I
urge you not to feel superior tho' I understand the creative impulses
which perhaps put one's feeling on a stage in which all of life can be
reenacted in a highly dramatic and tragic interpretation of it.*
*What is this mystical goal we attempt all our lives to reach? Is it not
simplicity? Then we cannot find it in the complex mazes of thought,
the sparring with overwhelming forces—the incessant battling against
overwhelming forces.*

*Flow with them and help those who fall staggered in the march. Give
your heart tangible proof of its goodness. Help those who are helpless—but do not tarry too tong at their aid—lest you become over
sympathetic and the march passes you by.*
*Do not expect to be helped. The strength of your own legs will carry you
forward—if the desire is great enough. There is no time for weakness.
You can rest at the end of the road.*
*By your picture it seems you've been taking life a bit seriously Ha! Ha!
Good grief! I indeed waste my life—perhaps it isn't worth anything
but an indolent waste. When will you stop playing for churches? When
will you tear away from conscious intellectual endeavor and begin to
live? Remember there is only one life, and it should be lived exploringly,
humorously, and to the full capacity of passion.*

*On this the aged mind can find fruit for happy thought and appraising
reminiscences. Always live with an eye to the future. I look forward to
returning and seeing you again—I will probably upset all your plans.
You write on your snapshot, "The church is St Johns Divine." A few
blocks away is the Academy of Design I attended, a thousand years*

*ago. I used to lose myself in the vast spiral staircases and I used to listen to the organ there (Gluck's Orpheus) in the church of course. You cannot imagine how happy I am that you have heard from Harold. I already wrote to him and also to Mother of having heard from him. I thought it was an occasion. I will not ask you about Rene. In my last letter to you I made plain that I do not wish her image to revive this smoldering pain she has imbedded within me. Under no circumstances do I wish to be reminded of her. She understood I wanted all of her or nothing—I am left with nothing. Let it be that way.*

*Yes I read Dorian Grey quite a time back. I enjoyed it immensely. I find it difficult to write to Joann—you see—I hardly know her—I've only seen her a few times if you remember—however—I will answer her letter. I do enjoy reading them but I feel that perhaps she writes from a sense of duty. I hope I am wrong. I should like to know how you live, activities, interests, appointments, places, etc.*
*Well, I'll say goodnite; I must for there are other things that fill me things coming from your world.*
*Have I been gone long? How long?*
*Please write again,*
*Affectionately,*
*Ugo*

*March 18, 1945*

*Dear Mother & Dad,*
*Here it is Sunday—long ago the day lost all meaning, but there's something special about today's Sunday—maybe it's the mood the weather is in, maybe it's me, recalling the sweetness of lost Sundays, or perhaps the lingering memory of some song I haven't heard in years. Across the road is a church. Artillery and bombs have added a grotesque touch to its original design. Churches always appear so*

*eternal so indestructible just like those lost Sundays—but I am looking at it now, with its guts spilled out, and the only thing I have of Sunday is a memory. The civilians wear their Sunday best; most of them are old people and very young people, occasional in between.*

*One wonders where they come from—the majority of houses are only rubble and shells, these people are not unhappy. 've seen them from the coasts of France to the Rhine—and these people who have suffered the hell of two armies who have had their nearest kin killed, whose houses are desolate ruins, who have no luxuries, eat black bread etc., etc.— These people are pale, timid, weary—unconscious of the fierce drama they are part of. These people are the people of the world, crushed, oppressed, yet they smile and wear their Sunday best, today.*

*An old woman and her daughter after much difficulty on my part to understand, explains that their father (the girls) is missing for three days. It could have been my own mother or sister asking me to help them. They asked whether he was killed by some Yank; these people expect anything and accept all. I took it upon myself to help them. In short time the matter was straightened their faces shone with gratitude they left. I'm writing—to tell you how wonderful to live for moments like this. Its so seldom one has the freedom to express love, war has out vogued it.*

*Walter has written and told me that Harold has finally sent you a letter—I know how relieved you must feel. And I guess I'm happiest when everybody else is happy. In case my letters don't arrive on time— here's wishing you and Pop and Ev, & Dick and Walter and Joann and little Dickey and of course Michael—Happy Easter for the third time on the same breath. And don't forget to let this one be a happy one!*
*Affectionately,*
*Always, Ugo*

*March 1945*

*Dear Folks!*
*Two days after the first meeting with Harold—I was again happily*
*surprised to see him once more. This time, I drove back with him and*
*spent the remainder of the evening and night with him.*

*This morning he went back to his original place for an indefinite time,*
*somewhere between Verdun and Metz. I wouldn't be surprised if he*
*arrived home before me. However there is another war to be fought*
*(like it or not) and not everyone will be coming home for discharge or*
*furlough. For myself I look forward to no new prospects. I am resigned*
*to accept what comes; I urged Harold to maintain the same attitude*
*thereby avoiding the sting of shattered hopes or disappointments.*
*Contrary to what you might believe we talked little but an inner*
*communication oscillated between ourselves. I probed him to release*
*(gradually) certain emotions I know to be harbored.*

*I think it was a bit difficult for both of us—but we finally cut the ice.*
*His main concern is Ann. It is difficult for one with his capacity to*
*love—to be separated. And this I feel, augmented by the fact that he*
*has a trying time translating his thoughts and emotions via letter. I*
*must write immediately to Ann about this. It would be unfair to both if*
*such a circumstance evolved itself into a basis for misunderstanding.*
*I am more strongly attached to him than ever before, we talked freely*
*and overleapt the superficial bias of personalities. It was brother to*
*brother with the mutual sympathies and longings of soldiers. Soldiers*
*have their own language (most of it, extreme invective) not at all like I*
*am writing—perhaps it is an emotional outlet, or stabilizer.*

*He is in the prime of health and has not varied a bit from his original*
*lovable manliness. He is in a good outfit, fine fellows to work with,*
*very indulgent. I was impressed and satisfied with the whole setup. I*
*know I shall have more peace of mind concerning his activities and*
*ultimate welfare. His life is far from hazardous if he remains with it.*

*I told him to inform me immediately if there were any changes. I do not expect any due to the importance of their work.*

*There are times when he cannot write due to the secrecy of his activities—remember this for the future; it should prove quite a consolation for you. I urged him to write often to you and pointed out the importance of constant writing to his wife I am sure that if he can he will, and only when he is so indisposed by a futile sense of longing and loneliness—will he permit himself to become indolent in his correspondence. You must exert more than the usual understanding. He is anxious to receive letters. Surely you will not fail.*

*He had nice living quarters—bed and kitchen included. We had fresh eggs and powdered milk concocted into a delicious eggnog. And from all descriptions his Luxembourg habitation is a soldier's dream. With movies and coffee and after hours. However—it's amazing how poor these substitutes become in the face of an ever-present longing for the nearness and embrace of someone beloved.*

*It is difficult to delineate the line where suffering begins or ends. I have my suspicions that Harold misses everyone of you more than he is prone to admit—nor is there lacking, that rare quality of boundless love, for you, in his character. Words are futile to describe the quiet melancholy I feel now saying, "so long kid!" to him—and knowing I will not see him again for months—perhaps more. I am writing of the impressions he gave me—and if these impressions convey to you the eternity of love and goodness he shines with—then your response should reach him in an abundance of mail.*

*We had many laughs and these inspired by a pair of wine bottles and the inevitable comic to be found in every group.*
*We had needless to say a happy time.*

*Of myself what can I say? Except that the letter I sent you previous to this one was filled with horrible emotion which if you cannot understand or believe you would please me by forgetting and ignoring its*

*contents. I assure you it was the maximum of indiscreetness and anger.*
*I do not forgive myself for complaining and making a fuss about things,*
*which I thought long ago I had learned to endure. I suppose the prob-*
*lem can be best ironed-out if we cease talking of it, writing of it, and*
*thinking of it. With your help (mom) I have allowed myself to imagine*
*the worse. And I suppose in the end you had no way of knowing that*
*I contained the most unreasonable type of passion for Rene. That one*
*part of me is absolutely (I confess) untouchable—and I am perfectly*
*calm when I say that (with all respect to my primitive instincts).*
*Somebody is going to feel very much hurt for stepping on my toes! The*
*time is ripe for me to assert myself—I'm going to live as I feel—and*
*not feel as I live. O.K.?*

*I've got to write to Ann now.*
*until the next letter Happy Easter and*
*remembrances to all*
*Affectionately,*
*Ugo*

*March 28, 1945*

*Dear Walt,*
*In answer to your letter of Mar 20 which arrived at a breath taking*
*pace I devote these sincerest sympathies tho' I find it increasingly diffi-*
*cult to write due primarily to the confusion of problems which by now*
*you are aware of.*

*The letters I have written home and to you and to Rene will have made*
*clear my attitude which weeks later has not altered. I am determined*
*to deal with this problem impartially, and personally letters bearing*
*discussion of it can never satisfy me or alleviate the attitude I now*
*maintain.*

*I have seen Harold: rather than repeat myself I urge you to read my impressions of that meeting which were written in a letter to Mom and a second one to Ann. My thanks to you and Joann for the pkg. of books just lately received—however my time is taken up at present with the discharge of certain duties.*

*Your letter in content deals with the eternal question of woman. Strife again between you and Joann. Perhaps maladjustment of a temporary nature. If it is any comfort to you to write of it to me then by all means do so—however I cannot afford suggestions or voice opinions.*

*In regards to your work: I am happy to hear you have left the cold interior of churches. With your ability I would get into the swing of things and join some orchestra. This is not a prostitution of art! Live as you want by extending feelers in all directions. Stop seeking inspiration where it doesn't abide. Meet people who have means and influence. See through the illusion of great art and you will have great art. Simplicity, roughness, abandonment of expression this is originality! Form your decisions by deciding, which will make you breathe easier. Don't, don't allow love to dictate—you do the dictating, the creating. Be the primary force in shaping your destiny—and you are the shaper of other destinies.*

*Experiment with things even if you have a preconceived idea that they will not bring you joy. You might be surprised!*

*Stop giving lessons, stop playing in churches, funerals—go out and get drunk!*

*Surely if you can't stand N.Y. leave it! It seems quite simple to me. And if Joann doesn't like Jersey let her stay in N.Y. This solves the problem physically, but as for your feelings don't give them powers to dictate happiness or sorrow to you.*

*Here I am winding up with a sermon it never fails! Damn.*

*Especially when my own life is such a blotch—but heavy pressure has drummed into me a peculiar aggressiveness and I am happy to report that I am free, no inhibitions of personality or of feeling, no convictions but they have been tested and tempered, equally sympathetic to fortune and misfortune. As gentle or as rough as required. I am myself. One can help control the ills of the world, but never cure them. I think perhaps you should seek achievement in finding your own soul—your own person. Who was it that said, "Know thyself." and you will know all. Of course I am not happy but then again it comes chiefly from the idea that we are all destined to die. And all of our living struggle appears futile, preposterous and if you have a sense of humor, ridiculous. Be less conscious of art—it will speak of itself. Absorb the natural, press your hands upon the rough bark of trees, lay in the grass and sleep. Awake knowing that you are as low as the lowest as high as the highest. Be not a representation of things but be those things. Cleanse yourself of the thoughts of dead men dead centuries—begin to feel, to breathe!*

*Am I conveying to you the idea that I know? I know nothing except that Heaven and Hell are both the living present—and tomorrow I shall be the stuff from which grass, weed and wild flowers will spring.*

*Let me spend myself in passion for life and not waste it on its representations. Let me end here.*

*Maybe I've been gone too long and people seem strange indeed.*

*Goodnite*

*As always,*

*Ugo*

*March 29, 1945*

*Crossed the Rhine—most impressive crossing. Crossed at a narrow point approx. 500 yrds. Entered Dinslaken—town pounded into rubble. Spent Easter here.*

*Chapter Eleven*

# APRIL 1945: THE RHINE AND THE ELBE RIVERS

## I AM COME HOME TO YOU

During this period the Military Police performed their usual activities, such as traffic control, prisoner of war evacuation, Division Command Post guard, and investigation. An attack was launched across the Dortmund-Ems canal on April 2. The canal was 30 feet deep, and about thirty five yards wide. "A thirty minute barrage of artillery paved the way. Enemy artillery and mortar fire harassed the men of the 29th. The troops waded knee deep in mud. Scaling ladders were thrown against the far wall. Once the 116th reached the far wall, enemy resistance slackened." (*The Long Line of Splendor*)

As the Germans retreated, thousands of displaced persons spilled out from their slave-labor camps, and there was mass confusion. The Ninth Army took control, and the 29th Division took full responsibility for this sector. From April 8 to 18, the Division was responsible for more than 72,000 displaced persons and 89 POW camps with more than 40,000 prisoners. These people were exhausted, hungry, and had to be deloused. All of the horrors of the Nazi regime that had been hidden away were now evident. Some of the 116th Regiment uncovered a slave-labor camp and witnessed the depravity of Hitler's policies. The 29th was eventually honored by the Holocaust Museum in Washington, D.C., for liberating this camp.

A pocket of German soldiers was caught between the Armies of the British and the Ninth Army. It was the task of the 29th to clear this pocket of resistance. On April 18 and 19, the 115th and 116th began the "mopping up" operations.(*Long Line of Splendor*)

There were 180 casualties in the Division for April.

In one of the drawings for April, a triumphant MP waving the convoys of men and material on the cleared open roads of Germany: Heading to Berlin. The 29th Division was now an occupying force.

*April 20, 1945*

*[Rene]*

*Soon, very soon I am coming home. I feel this as something I cannot explain.*

*You will be the first person I see when you write send me your phone no. Remember—that I have been gone a long time. Remember also that I have been away fighting a war—and that I may appear a bit strange. However I appear to you no matter what expression is frozen on my countenance, no matter what I may say, Remember that I am come home to you. And that the boy or man you see in uniform loves you—as the beat of his very heart. Take care of him he will make you a princess. He will make you live forever!*

*I have been under a very severe strain.*

*For almost one year I have had artillery fired at me. I am not completely myself.*

*I have been strafed and fired upon—and my comrades have fallen dead beside me. Always I have been on the front line. wondering why I am alive.*

*If I ever receive a wound.*

*Do not worry because I live for you and as long as I am conscious I know I am fighting for your life! I will not fail you! Remember this—remember this! And know that I am happy since you have accepted my love at last.*

*Trust me please, Give me strength*

*I am tired.*

*Gogo*

*On the move.*

*April 26, 1945*

*My Darling Rene,*
*From your letter of April 18, which arrived today, I learn, with remorse*
*and sorrow that you have not yet received my letters which will tell you*
*that everything is all right.*

*Whatever unhappiness I suffer is that which I have so regretfully*
*inflicted upon you. Here I have received all of your assurances, your*
*explanations while at this moment, as I write, as I think of you, you are*
*still in that terrible abyss. I wish I would fly to your heart and pick you*
*up in my arms. The love I feel for you rises above my mortal limitations*
*and what perhaps is that grain of hope you feel even now is it not my*
*own spirit giving you reason to hold on? In letters, so much depends*
*upon Time, yet the urgency of our thoughts must destroy this barrier!*
*You know you know how we both have tried to lift to its ultimate that*
*existing bondage between us. And I feel sure that this has helped*
*preserve it during these years, against creeping inconsistencies of our*
*age. I will never, as I once said before, allow the flame rest. If it was a*
*spark, we blew it into flame, and it must mount higher, higher, higher,*
*through the years until there are no more years.*

*There are and have been few people who have sounded to the very*
*depths of their personalities the love idea. Modestly I include you and I.*
*The large souls, the creators, the thinkers, the poets the accepted giants*
*these upon recognizing the flame, felt its power and found their voices.*
*Their voices shout to us now and we listen to the song it is all there is of*
*Heaven.*

*I know as surely you know that we are incredibly mated of the same*
*temperament physically, psychically, and as such I may know more of*
*you than it is necessary for you to say or for me to confess. Likewise*
*you know me more than we both admit. This then is why we both have*
*felt the same things, written as we have written. I understand why you*
*wished to say good-bye (but it was, my darling, most inopportune and*

*inconsiderate of you to write it) and did you not imagine that I would lose my head when others kept telling me weird things about you? You see, I coupled what you had written to Sam; your wish to say good-bye written to me, malicious gossip from others about you, my own strain, and I all but went nuts! Because I hold it sacred to me, your love, I can prove most unreasonable when I imagine it to be a mere bauble of the concept. I do not think I am jealous. It is rooted deeper than this word, and I think, tho my explanation only suggests it, that you know clearly what I mean since you feel identically about me.*

*Knowing then how we basically feel about one another, we must begin to recognize and allow freedom to our separate desires. We must allow for a few disagreements, but it will be a pleasure to straighten them out in the future. I will take this attitude, that if there is ever anything I wish to do and you feel strongly against it, I will not do it. And we will find a compromise always.*

*When I wrote the word "deceive" to you! I did not mean it to its ultimate degree. My God! Never that! I did mean, that I was led to believe that other lips had touched yours and other arms were arousing the sleeping butterflies. This latter was not a sleeping suspicion I secretly held nor was it of my own imagination. It was told me point blank—it was easy to surmise the rest. Yet all this did not occur at all, except in the sense you described, namely that of fraternal caressing. Do not think me crude if I tell you that I do not want this to happen again. Dick has placed me in a difficult position—so difficult that I will be unable to write to him until I see him. He will never as long as he lives be able to explain his conduct towards you nor his letter describing that episode; you see he did not describe it as a fraternal embrace, but as a passionate one. I sicken with anger when l think of it! Do not even try to defend him—it would be psychologically a misstep for you. I suppose it is best if you understand this and abide by this. That it is wisest if we no longer discuss this situation—until I return. Letters are inadequate indeed!*

*There are certain things I do not want to know about now nor try to understand—understanding is not always consoling.*
*I repeat with strong emphasis. Do not attempt a reconciliation with members of my family. Whatever letters I write them now will not contain even the slightest suggestion of you and I or our problems.*
*It will be as you wished and as I strongly feel that our business is our own.*

*Those who hear evil gossip from place to place harm themselves eventually.*
*And don't you worry my darling. I'll stick by!*
*P.S. I'm sending you a bottle of perfume. I had no choice in picking it; you may not like it. Let me know if by lucky chance it falls with your taste.*

*Love Always,*
*XXX and X*

*April 27, 1945*

*My answer to yours of April 12.*
*I don't know where to begin. You ask me to clarify my present attitude in not uncertain terms. It is easy for you, surrounded with all the comforts of life, to respond impetuously and not without the lash to my own notes. The strain is great and I am weary. Time heals and I am grateful. If you have a duplicate letter of the 12th, lay it in front of you and compare notes. In any event I trust to your memory.*

*Wait, I wonder now. Yes, it is no use. Battle it you will my love and doubt it. I cannot help that. What more can I say? You don't realize what a tremendous word censorship is. If you did you would not question me or what I am doing. Look, I work seven days in a week—there is no end! Sometimes, night and day. I work outside with heavy equipment in every weather. I wear an iron hat (because I detested hats!). I walk and walk till one's legs feel like stumps. My head is made of soft clay from obeying orders. These letters are censored by my own Company. The last vestige of individuality and truth must be stripped from them. I am furiously humbled!*

*I do not care to write under these restrictions—yet I must. Consider if you please this aggravating condition.*

*You certainly help my peace of mind! I must tell you someday how nice it was to receive letters that told me I lied—while I was in Hell!*

*What a child you are—better that way—I love you that way.*

*If you wish, I won't write anymore, only don't threaten me. If you wish we will discontinue our communications except for an occasional message saying you are still waiting and that I still love you. Only stop questioning me. Remember the vow I made? Well you ridiculed it once too often. Forget it! You doubted my love once too often. I am a fool for repeating it. Push if you must everything to the darkness. I can bear it. Like so much sweat and tears. My mother and father, the thought of them growing older and older I may never see them when I come back. Tear down the walls of, power! For my patience has reached its end! And I pray for tomorrow when I can release this fury.*

*April 29, 1945*

*My Darling Rene,*

*Another letter arrived dated April 19. From its contents I again gather that you have not been receiving my letters. This knowledge is painful; the thought of you suffering so horribly only because my messages are dead things packed in the hold of a ship. And here you surmise that my silence, which is not mine at all, gives you disdainful answers to all these courageous letters you have written me.*

*Perhaps, and I pray you may have received at least one of my letters and that this note comes only to augment and beseech you to accept the complete faith and trust I have in you. I urge you to cease writing of this mad state of things—I want no further explanation of your conduct—it is simply that you have denied the evil gossip against you; you have said to me, "It was not so," and I believe you.*

*Contrary to what you have expressed to me, everything is not against you. Then you know Dick has written me! Don't be alarmed, my Darling. They are not hurting you; they are hurting me, but then, I am slightly immune. I often wonder why they insist upon destroying my concept of you. What are the motives behind it? They have described you to me as a cheap five and dime sex book describes its heroine. "She shamelessly tells smutty jokes, she smokes, she"—and a host of misplaced adjectives. The whole thing is fantastic! After nearly three years of not seeing you—and weakened by the pressures of war, I was for a moment ready to believe anything. Only a terrible rage seized me in time; that others dare mention all this with the breath of you, whom I have lived for, whom I have built my life and reason to life upon, why? why? Where do they find basis for the accusations? How can they possibly lie, so unashamed? Do they think I will not return to face them? They are wrong! I will return, and when I do someone must pay for these three years of uncertainty!*

*You must do as I tell you to do! You are not to see anyone except Walt and Joann. This includes the entire family, and any others! Upon my return, I will meet with this problem; it will be dealt with as I see fit. I suppose you know how I feel, "That I am grieved deeply knowing of how ill you have been and are from some chronic disorder." Is it truly a serious cause? Please, for our sake, do all you can to keep well. We haven't begun to live yet.*

*Forever yours,*
*Ugo*

*Chapter Twelve*

---

# MAY 1945:
# UNCENSORED MEMORIES

---

## WAR'S END: THE ELBE RIVER LINE

The Germans were on the east side of the River Elbe, and the 29th had a defensive line on the west side. The International Boundary had been pre-established. The Americans would not enter Berlin, or cross the Elbe. The Russians had entered Berlin, and were now approaching the Elbe River. For the 29th Division, the war was virtually over. The German troops were eager to surrender to the Americans, rather than the Russian army. "Early in the morning of May 2 outposts could look across the river and see the German soldiers laying out the white flags on the east bank." By 9:00 p.m., 6,700 prisoners of war surrendered; the final count for the day was more than 10,000 men. On May 2, members of the 175th Regiment made contact with the Russian Army. (*29 Let's Go*) The fighting was over. Hitler had committed suicide, and Berlin lay in ruins. The task of rebuilding lives was about to begin.

*May 1945*

*[Rene,]*

*As I write I find it difficult to realize that I am not censored. Words just won't come now. I've been tongue-tied so long.*

*Perhaps if you write me questions I will loosen up a bit. O.K.? I am still in the 29th doing occupation work in Bremen—my work for some time*

*revolved about divisions traffic system (after all, I am a copper) ha!*
*Isn't that a gag!*
*Training with the infantry in England was tougher than combat. Of*
*course they taught us commando tactics, but they never suggested a*
*real enemy. (He makes all the difference.) I used to be a doggie with a*
*B.A.R. I assure you I would have been dead by now—if as I wrote you*
*once while in England (I was expecting a change for the better).*
*I didn't realize how much better until shortly after D-Day. I haven't*
*killed anybody yet, I don't think so??*
*Most of the real killing is done by artillery. I have been so terrified as to*
*forget eating for days at a time.*

*Once in Brest, France, a shell landed four yds. in back of me (four*
*feet to be exact) I measured it next day. It was a dud or I wouldn't*
*be writing about it. On D+4, I was in a field with the Rangers—Jerry*
*bombed and strafed us—a few of the boys were replaced by craters*
*(approx. 10 ft. from me). I didn't display any heroics until it was abso-*
*lutely necessary—and it was on D-Day (I spotted a half dozen mines)*
*and by lying down parallel to them I cautioned the infantry as they*
*approached. The doggies used to be in back of me in those first days.*
*(I shouted at them but one guy didn't hear, and I saw him sink a few*
*yds. from me; his legs were only pieces of wet flesh and clothes; the*
*blast was only one of many.)*

*Rene, I'm safe now; you don't mind if I talk a bit? That's enough for a*
*while. Yes one war is enough and sooner or later one's number comes.*
*For as far as I could see along the water's edge there were bodies,*
*hundreds, hundreds dead—I didn't believe it then—I still can't quite*
*grasp it. How did I come through it without a scratch?*
*This is a terrible letter! There were a lot of funny incidents too. I'll tell*
*you all someday.*
*Goodnite and*
*Love always,*

*May 22, 1945*

*Dear Mother,*
*Sorry I haven't written for so long—in fact I rarely write to anyone.*
*There is no particular reason for this other than lack of incentive. This*
*perhaps covers multitudinous reasons if one cares to search for them.*
*I think perhaps the grim excitement of war is wearing off, and I am*
*taking life as it comes. I am doing less introspective and retrospective*
*thinking—beyond this I cannot explain my feelings; whatever they are*
*they do not suggest intensity—and I am quite relieved.*

*I have been gone much too long to miss anyone with any particular*
*longing—excuse me for being frank. Existence here, prolonged and*
*intense, has finally rooted itself within me and become life.*
*Even as I write the war has ended, or rather extinguished itself like a*
*candle burning beyond its wax and igniting the wooden holder—fool-*
*ishly resisting its inevitable death.*

*I've lived a thousand lives, and I've died many. I have changed-in so*
*far as I am free—yes, I am truly free mentally and spiritually. I have*
*none of the thinking, which encumbers or enslaves me. I have none of*
*the values and relative perspectives, which civilians abide by. I don't*
*want them; they are one-sided and painful to bear. I am free! I have*
*lived in mansions and also in holes and filthy cellars. I am an eagle*
*looking out and below from my high cliff, and I see a vain, futile,*
*hopeless procession of insignificant activity moving dismally and*
*aimlessly across the face of the earth; a caravan bound by ignorance*
*and fettered with illusions.*

*I am conscious of my own vanity, and I laugh at the world's. At least I*
*am conscious of my limitations and reasons, my pride and my humil-*
*ity, my strength and my weakness; at least I know that I am also as*
*insignificant as the least of these, and as significant as the best of*
*them. Paupers and Kings both can be leveled into each other, as I have*

*witnessed. When I have finished paying my debt to society for allowing me the privilege of living the life endowed upon me by society, I will live it as an individual with all the might of body and soul. With all the freedom which belongs to the chainless spirit! I will not bow to custom, to tradition, to laws written and unwritten, to creeds, religions, ethics; they are for me created.*

*I expect to come home when they send me home. One needs 85 pts. for a discharge. I have 82 pts. which means I will either stay here for an indefinite occupation or return home for a furlough and then well, maybe the Pacific. One learns not to trust to optimism in the Army. However I am of the opinion that total peace is not too far in the offing. And I feel that this year sometime I will be home. I am in the best of health and have no real reason for being discouraged except for tiring of the uncertain future.*

*The censorship of letters has been lifted—and it is a great comfort to realize this new freedom.*

*At the present writing I am in Bremen, Germany. Perhaps I will remain here for a few months as rumor has it. Men of the division have already left for home. We are living in houses.*

*I've got my own room, bed, table, and clothes rack.*

*I am in the center of a small town named Vegesack.*

*War has passed it by. All day I work with maps over a real drawing table I set up in the living room.*

*Time is passing slowly now since most of the excitement of war has ended.*

*Its not too late, is it, to know that I remembered you on Mother's Day? Please take care of yourself and Dad—and send my affections to Dick and Evelyn and Dicky. I wonder what Harold is doing?*

*Regards to Michael.*

*Ever loving*
*Yours,*
*Ugo*

*May 25, 1945*

*My Beloved,*
*I am coming home perhaps before autumn, perhaps later, perhaps*
*sooner. I think in the near future.*
*It's a matter of a few months. Perhaps only weeks; then it will be*
*days—and then hours.*

*I have 87 points and a possible discharge. They gave us another*
*campaign star for Central Europe. This raised me over the hump! I*
*have one for Normandy, one for Northern France, and one for Rhine-*
*land. I made it without "purple hearts." I made it without a scratch! In*
*the face of moments of certain death, I always believed I would return.*
*I used to say: She's waiting for you, suffering and living for you; if*
*you will it, have faith in yourself, remember you are invulnerable. I am*
*coming home pretty much the same fellow as when I left. But I will*
*need you for a real friend, a real companion, there isn't anyone I know*
*to greet me—the few friends I left behind in U.S. have gone their way.*
*I brought you home from the hospital once—now it's your turn to escort*
*me home. Send me your phone no. and I will give you a ring. Would it*
*be best if I waited for you to come first—or should I walk right up to*
*your house? If I get drunk, I will ride down Sanford St. on a white stal-*
*lion like I told you when we were kids. (But I can't ride!) I'm liable to do*
*anything, you know. What will you wear? How will you look? What will*
*we talk of? Perhaps my first words will be "Take that hat off, it looks*
*like a pumpkin." Ha! and if I say "you look nice," you will probably tell*
*me I am lying or something. (I request you use little if any greasepaint)*
*and please wear a little Djerkiss, like you used to.*
*It's really late now and I must hit the sack (literally, I have a sack).*
*P.S. Send me a pair of good sunglasses and a hat that looks like this.*

*Goodnite*
*Love*
*Auf Wiederschen*

*Chapter Thirteen*

---

# JUNE 1945:
# THE AFTERMATH

---

The war was over. Ugo was stationed near Bremen, in a small town called Vege-sack. He had time to contemplate, and begin to unravel the mess created by his family and Rene. It would take years of anguish and vacillation. The truth differed depending upon who told the story. A question mark still hangs in the air, even sixty years later. The relationship was torn apart, and these two dear people didn't have a chance to experience a life together or to experience the natural progress of a first love.

The war and its memories remained dormant and compartmentalized, somewhere in Ugo's unconscious. Not until 1984 did Omaha and D-Day return to be recreated in his art for posterity to see. In January of 1993, Ugo was hospitalized with pulmonary fibrosis, barely reathing, unable to walk; each morning that I entered his hospital room he had awoken from his dreams of landing on Omaha Beach, shouting to his comrades, "You've been shot, get away from the Obstacle, it's a target." Ugo's final "landing" was January 31, 1993.

*June 1, 1945*

*Dear Walt,*
*Stepping aside from the usual tiresome channel of thoughts expressed*
*in letters I have a confession to make. For years I have been unable to*
*read without myself being consumed with the desire to also make myself*

*heard. In brief, the very sight of a book excites me, arouses long dormant aspirations, creates in me the impulse to assert, pronounce, declare and more—to infuse my response to life in a concrete, tangible form,—yes, to write, to translate myself above the perishable dust I am—to hew out of the indifferent rock of existence a niche—to claim my affinity with conscious things and so preserve my right to life—to prove or at least justify the existence of a soul.*

*In this small way—I can help mankind attain a reason to live.*
*I will never be happy until someone places a little book in my hand and the author reads:*
*"Giannini."*
*I will cherish and try to uphold whatever confidence and encourage-ment you think worthy of me.*
*Please write in answer.*

*Here I am in Vegesack, a small town near Bremen, Germany—for the present serving in an occupational capacity—the Germans regard American M.P.s as S.S. troopers—I certainly won't break down and laugh. Their illusions make me impregnable. Ha! Ha!*
*Of course they ask me if I am American. I tell them: "I was fostered by a tribe of aboriginals who befriended me when I was a child." This they accept as fact. Europeans are naive to the point of ignorance. Non-frat-ernization rules prevent me from becoming over-friendly, at the same time hindering my chances of learning a bit of Kraut talk. However— my work does permit certain duties to be also privileges.*

*I've got an excellent camera, a 35mm. Can you get me some film? Might as well dispatch that cigarette lighter you promised to send—I don't know how long I will be here. When that fourth star becomes official, I will have 87 points and a possible discharge. (I feel confident.) I went sailing on the Weser R. (only a few yards from me) the other day. I like it fine—got all-naked and lay in the bottom of the craft; sun felt good indeed. I didn't try swimming yet—waters a bit dirty and I'm a bit nervous of water now. (I'll get over it.)*

*I live in a small house, electricity, a radio, and a bed (no sheets). Before the civilians left, they asked me to please water the plants daily. (I am devoted to this haus frau task.) Might as well inject this piece of past history: I had suffered one week of battle neurosis while we gave Brest (France) a work over. The Jerries turned their 300 mm naval guns at us; two landed in my back yard; a huge hunk of shrapnel tore a window in my pup tent (as if I wasn't getting enough ventilation!). To make matters worse our own P47s bombed and strafed our area; we had a lot of fun (now that it's over). And now, night comes and I listen—no planes, no shells, no chattering machine guns, no footsteps, no twigs cracking—I used to dig a foxhole every night and sweat out the thought, Is it a foxhole or a grave? How I wished I was a moron then—my imagination only made matters worse. I wasn't afraid of dying—only leaving people waiting wasn't a nice thought—and I hated to feel that I was a sucker! Every time I saw a dead Yank I'd think, He used to write letters too.*

*I'm interested to know what's going on back there.*
*What is Joann doing?*
*How is Rene?*
*What are you engaged in now? Piano lessons and more study?*
*How are Mom and Pop? Tell them I'll drop in one of these days, and if they don't recognize me it's the moustache. (I shaved it off a few times but I felt lost without it.) I think its here to stay.*
*I wrote to Dick.*
*How about sending me a package?*
*1 jar of peppers*
*(Mama knows) pckg. Dried olives*
*1 can caponatina salami*
*dried figs and other knickknacks*
*I have a premonition I might be home before my pckg. arrives.*
*But then I base my optimism on wishful thinking.*
*Auf Wiederschen*

*As Ever,*
*Ugo*

*July 7, 1945*

*Dear Walt,*

*Received your V Mail of June 26—I am answering immediately. Happy to hear that everyone at home is well.*

*However it is not happy to think that Harold must remain occupied with the business of war. I would have made an effort to have him transferred into my division when I last saw him—but I think he realized the lesser of two evils. The 29th has been an assault division and even tho' it is an occupation force now—the exigencies of war can very easily call upon it to assume its previous combat status.*

*Harold is a member of a dummy organization. They have equipment, which deals with psychological warfare—I inquired personally into it, and I feel safe in saying that he will return unharmed. In any event it is of inestimable importance and necessity that he receive constantly the comfort of letters—even tho' they remain unanswered. Speaking from simple experience, I cannot stress this enough. The hardest thing for a soldier is to endure endless loneliness and monotony—The mind becomes a blank. For myself, the strain of war is lifting slowly but surely, and I feel with quiet joy the thought of resuming civilian life—It does not alarm me—I embrace whatever struggles it will present. They cannot be compared with or ever mentioned with the same breath of the past struggles. The business of swimming a lake is quite simple to one accustomed to the fury of the oceans.*

*I am also preparing to return. There is nothing ill that I feel now which will not be forgotten by the grace of a few hours' peace and sunlight. I am in the best of health. I say this without reservation and I have planned on a continuance of it. When one has health and freedom, one has all. I have absolutely no reason to be pessimistic—anyone can be that. We should spend more time laughing and enjoying the good things.*

*Did I lose any hair? In my case a high forehead doesn't denote over-whelming mental powers—and I can't blame heredity alone, ha! Speaking of my vanity I will say I've certainly thinned out and stranger than all—my hair is crinkly like a Negroes. I look 30, think 40, and would like to be 15 again. I'm 25, and eligible for discharge, marriage,—or more war. What have you?*

*I am indeed becalmed—only sporadic and uncertain traces appear of an inner and previous intensity. It seems now that I am beginning to feel my boyhood reflections. What were then vague and disquieting uncertainties have now become firm convictions. I am East Orange, the schools, the art classes, the books consumed slowly, the walks with Rene, the music you played, the poems I read, the sunlight and the rain the little room burning a late candle for the acquisition of understanding and the peace I sought to problems; I am the agony of the war and its survivor, I am the endurance of endless physical, spiritual and mental flagellation. I am cleansed; I am free like a butterfly burst from its prison of sluggish existence within its cocoon. I am happy in the things which wilt be forever hidden from eyes that do not seek these secret joys. You cannot impress sight upon a blind man, but you can hold to his nostrils the fragrance of flowers—this you can do.*
*I do toy with the possibility of being home within a few months. Rumors fly fast and thick—but I am ready at all times.*
*Love to all and send*
*My usual best to Mom and Pop.*

*Affection,*
*Ugo*

# Chapter Fourteen

# 1989-1993:
# RETURN TO H-HOUR
# THE CONTEMPORARY WORKS

## WHY? WHY?

In 1993, January 30—the day before Ugo died—he cried out: "Get me my bullet. For God's sakes let me die like a man!" Pete and Helen were there, and we tried to calm him down, the ravings of a sick man, so out of context. Mark, on the other hand, knew where the bullet was and was ready to help Ugo with his plan. It was in those moments, that Ugo revealed his true state of mind; a facet that had lain dormant since he brought that bullet back from the war in 1945.

The men of the 29th Division whom I had met, carried with them some indelible memories etched into their psyches, never to be forgotten. There was a fatalistic, superstitious view of life and death—"Your number's up—There's an Angel guarding you—The Joker's appeared." They had a sense of an otherworldly destiny. For Ugo: The bullet. The one with his name on it—it missed him, for all his time in battle. Now he would take it home. If he could keep it—he'd survive, and this he did. And on that day, January 30, 1993 he knew—there was no more time. Death called to him, and he responded, but at the very last gasp at least he could die as a soldier—as a man—by the bullet; which was to him "ate" or fate.

He once said to me in those last days, "Morphine is for old ladies." Pretty funny—but I missed the point, the essence of his thinking and feeling. The guy was a soldier, a warrior, a man, and an artist.

It is in this context that one must decipher these contemporary works. Just as the very first drawings were made on Omaha in 1944, under completely impossible conditions—so were the last works made in 1992.

With oxygen being pumped into his lungs, no breath left. Once again, impossible to conceive of the courage he needed to create this final tribute to the 29th Division, the 116th Regiment.; Ugo's comrades in arms.

Ugo's hands creating and completing the full circle of his epiphany—in war.

## LIST OF ART WORKS

*Agony at Vierville* collage-mixed media 1986

*Obstacle, Seawall, H-Hour, D-Day* collage-mixed media; 47" × 64" 1988

*Metal Cross for Sergeant X* pastel 1991

*Requiem St. Lo; Normandy, France* pastel-paint 1991; 7-18-44 23" × 36"

*Omaha Beach, D Day* gesso-collage  1991

*The 29th* pastel 1992; 19" × 25"

*Ruins* collage 1992

*H-Hour* pastel 1992; 23" × 17"

*Requiem, Omaha Beach, D-Day, June 6, 1944*

## AGONY AT VIERVILLE

In June of 1984, Ugo was asked to give a lecture by his dear friend Francois Haymann. This was to be a presentation for the ROTC of Verona, New Jersey. Ugo began reading and researching. He read and reread *The Longest Day* by Cornelius Ryan and *Overlord* by Max Hastings. Many passages were underlined or triple checked. "Yet although the defenders (Germans) possessed the capability to maul the American landing on Omaha seriously, to impede and to disorganize it, they lacked the power to halt it absolutely. Despite the near total destruction of the first wave" of invaders landing on the western flank below Vierville–despite the casualties and the terror inflicted upon thousands of green troops, a great many men survived to reach the sea wall alive--enough, finally, to swamp the vastly outnumbered German defenders."[1] Forty years after D Day Ugo began to relive these events.

This extraordinary work was completed in 1986. *Agony at Vierville*, the images of war, now abstract. A cross covering the globe; a nail, representing the Crucifixion; the strip of land, torn and covered in blood are all part of the symbolism signifying Vierville on June 6th. The subdued and sorrowful colors speak of what occurred that terrible morning, June 6, 1944.

1. Hastings, Overlord, 97

# OBSTACLE: SEA WALL H-HOUR D-DAY
## *Collage 47" × 64"*

Ugo created this work in 1986, forty-two years after the invasion of Normandy. A lifetime had been lived in the interim: studies at the Art Student's League and with Fernand Léger in Paris; his subsequent marriage and children. Twenty-five years of teaching at Caldwell College for women (later to change to coed status), there was nearly complete silence about World War II. Like almost all of the Veterans of WWII the memories of their service lay buried deep within them. Omaha Beach on June 6, 1944 changed Ugo and his comrades completely. But there were no words, no memorials in the United States, no way to appease the pain of what each man had experienced.

In 1944 the Generals of Hitler were in disagreement about how to counter what they knew was about to happen; the invasion of Fortress Europe by the Americans and their allies. Rommel, known as the Desert Fox was convinced that the invasion would occur in Normandy. He systematically fortified the beaches at a frantic pace. There were thousands of mines. "Numerous obstacles had been laid under water - some of these were stakes carrying an antitank mine at the tip, others were concrete tetrahedrons, equipped with either steel blades or antitank mines- Up to May 13 a total of 517,000 foreshore obstacles were laid, of which 31,000 were armed with mines."[1] Rommel felt that the invading force had to be dislodged from the beach in 48 hours, or the war was over. As the Generals laid plans, Omar Bradley sent the 29th Division, 116 Regiment into the first wave. These men had never seen battle before. They were referred to by the Generals as unblooded troops. What followed was true chaos. But after the initial slaughter, and panic, each remaining soldier picked himself up and made his way off the beach, and fought his way, an inch at a time through Normandy.

Rommel, shortly after his defeat in Normandy, was forced to commit suicide by Hitler. By 1986 Bradley was dead; the men of the 116th had died or were dying. Ugo, diagnosed with pulmonary fibrosis, created a monument: *Obstacle, Sea Wall*. The surface of the dark water is slashed by a diagonal; the experience, which had no memorial, now captured in a monumental painting by a lowly private.

1. The Desert Fox In Normandy, S.W. Mitcham, Jr.  P. 20

# METAL CROSS FOR SGT. X
*Pastel 1991 25" × 31 ½"*

In the summer of 1992 the war works were framed. Specific titles were selected
for them, and in some instances dates were indicated. For this work, *Metal Cross
for Sgt. X*, the date: 6/7/44. A place: Isigny. Who was the Sergeant? Once more,
the symbols depict the battle scene. The stripes for the Sergeant, the arrows for
the battle, the Yin and Yang symbol was the 29th Division's insignia, the German
helmet, the German cross as well as the cross for the fallen men.

In the book *Maryland in WWII* volume I was this description: "On the narrow coastal strip near Grandcamp a group of Germans in a strategic position pinned down the 116th's men despite strenuous efforts to jar loose the enemy with rifles, grenades, tank and bazooka fire. Then Technical Sergeant Frank D. Peregorey of Charlottesville, Va., with hand grenade, rifle and bayonet killed eight Nazis, captured three others and destroyed the machine gun nest, which had delayed the 116th's advance. Grandcamp fell. Sgt. Peregorey was killed in action six days later. Isigny was seized two days later on the 9th."

## REQUIEM ST. LO
## NORMANDY FRANCE JULY 18, 1944

St. Lo, a vital communications center had to be taken. Between the troops of the 29th Division and the town were some seven miles of checkerboard fields and orchards edged with man made fences of brambles piled four to seven feet high. These were called hedgerows. They dated back to Caesar's time. The pre-invasion training had not prepared the men for this serious situation. The Germans took shelter to set up gun positions and snipers' nests so that each 100 yards was covered by enemy fire. On July 18, 1944 a special group of motorized 29th units occupied St. Lo after severe house-to-house fighting. After six weeks of continuous fighting the 29th had formed the cutting edge from the beaches of Normandy to St. Lo.[1]

In 1991 forty-seven years after the battle for St. Lo, Giannini created the Requiem for St. Lo; delicate and muted grays and gray blues, dusty blacks. The Yin and Yang symbol of the 29th Division, the crosses for suffering and death, the German Cross, the gravestones scattered almost randomly across the picture plane unite to create a haunting composition. One doesn't send an artist into battle for naught.

1. Maryland in WWII

# OMAHA BEACH, D-DAY

### *6/6/44 gesso 1991 38" x50"*

Petra ten Doesschate Chu, an art historian, wrote of Ugo's late works: "In 1986, feeling the first symptoms of the illness that would cause his death in 1993, he started a series of monumental works commemorating the Normandy offensive. Was it an homage to his former friends who never lived the full life he had lived, himself? Or else a final reckoning with an event that would still haunt his feverish brain during the last days of his life. *Agony at Vierville, Metal Cross for Sgt. X, Hinge Crucifix,*--works that combine drawing in various media with collage, are the distilled essence of Ugo's war experience. Chronicles written in symbolic signs--numbers (116, 29) letters (H Hr), arrows, crosses, flags, Uniform stripes, the yin-yang symbol of the 29th division--they contain the full experience of the war, just as the notes and symbols in a musical score contain within them the full sound of a symphony."

Omaha Beach, D-Day is a work that creates a deep and somber mood. It helps to know the history of the 29th Division. But without knowing any of the details of the Normandy Invasion, one knows that this work stands for those men lost in battle. The cross, to symbolize the suffering, to dignify the agony of all men, the arrows, for landing, the x's for the obstacles that ensnared so many, even before landing, the imprint of an actual soldier's boot, the blood stains to tell of Bloody Omaha, unite to create an elegy which will last beyond the death of the 29th Division's Infantry soldiers.

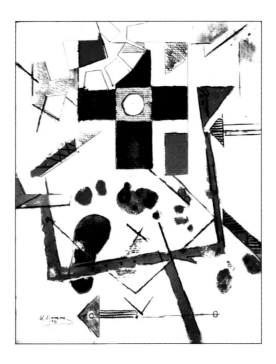

## THE 29TH
*Pastel 20"x 26"*

The Yin Yang sign was the insignia of the 29th Division. Maj. General Charles H. Gerhardt led this Division. A Division consists of about 14,000 men. The Division was divided into three regiments, 115th, 116th and 175th. Each Regiment consisted of 3,119 men. It was said of General Gerhardt that he had a regiment on the battlefield, a regiment in the hospital, and a regiment killed in action. This was not quite accurate, as by the end of the war the Division had been replaced by one hundred forty percent. (More than 20,000.) In the month of June 1944, the total killed in action were 1,154 men. 2,834 were wounded, 133 injured, 565 missing, and the total was 4,685. On June 6, 1944, June 7, 1944 there were 771 men killed or wounded in action, from the 116th Regiment. The 116th Regiment landed in the first assault on Omaha Beach. In this pastel the arrows represent points of landings, the Cross for death and suffering, the red of the bloody shore. Ugo created this composition when he was seventy-two, knowing full well that his life was ending. His hands created a memorial for those comrades who lived and died, on that day, and for those who lived and died in his heart and memory.

## RUINS
*Collage 1992*

*Ruins* represent the devastation that war leaves behind. Each time a battle ensues, each time a counter attack occurs, all living things are in peril; the civilian population, the animals, the plants, the houses, the churches, the monuments, the museums, all the treasures of the living are decimated. The language of war tries to obfuscate what actually happens; in the case of civilian casualties or unintended bombing of your own forces, the words used were "collateral damage." Cities pounded into rubble, civilians hiding in cellars, unintended victims.

In 1997, I visited a French farmhouse in Moyen where the American forces and the Germans had engaged in battle. The family hid in the cellar for days; when they were able to emerge the house was gone, the soldiers dead around them, and to this day they still find arms, mines, shells, as they continue to plow their fields.

*Ruins* smolders. It illustrates a planet no longer inhabitable: barren, stark, dead.

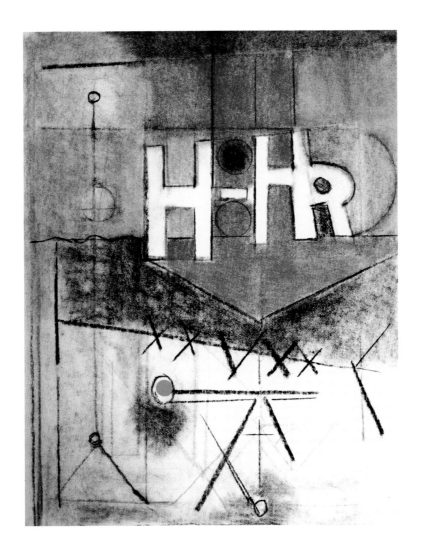

# H - H O U R
*Pastel 17" × 24", 1992*

In *H-Hour* we see an arrow, red; the invading force, the red of battle. The Xs indicating the obstacles. These were placed by the enemy to prevent boats from landing. The dot of Green, for Dog Green, the code for the sector in which the 116th Regiment was to land. This was one of the last works done by Ugo. He was on oxygen, and after October 5th, 1992 was not able to walk downstairs to the first floor. His studio was a large bedroom on the second floor of his home, and as long as he had any strength he continued to create these works. He created sketches for an entire series, entitled OMAHA. *H-Hour* symbolizes the artist struggling with the immensity of the initial landing in Normandy, the chaos and destruction experienced by each man, enemy and ally alike. It also refers to Ugo's understanding of his own mortality, his own struggle with death, his own personal H-Hour.

*Afterword*

# "GIANNINI'S BOOK"

By Maxine Giannini

I wake up in the middle of the night crying. Psychologists talk of "closure," one gets on with life, what's done is done, dead is dead. The living must go on. But, like Marley's Ghost, you came to haunt me. You rattled your chains from another place, another time. "The war is not my concern," I said.

"Humanity is your concern" was your cry—till I shook.

Yes, you haunted me. There were too many unexplained coincidences. The car that cut in front of me at Kennedy Airport with the license plate UGO, as I left to attend the 50th Anniversary of D-Day. Your drawings would be exhibited in Paris and on Omaha Beach. The name "DRUMMOND" that came to me while I was traveling on the bus to visit the American cemetery in Coleville-sur-Mer. Drummond's grave was there. He was a fellow M P. I found out in 1999 from Rex Potts that you, Drummond, and Rex were the last three to jump from your boat, Drummond was on your right, and was killed in the water, within minutes of that jump. I laid flowers at his grave in 1994. I was with a French Major who was in the French Reenactment Army, he dressed as an American M.P., and we became friends.

The second time I returned to France, in 1997, I traveled to Brest. I was traveling with a group of 29ers. Once again we followed the route of the war, Omaha, Issgny, St. Lo, Vire, Brest. We stayed in a dreary hotel in Brest. I met Joseph Balkoski, the historian who wrote *Beyond the Beachhead, The 29th Infantry Division in Normandy*. I showed him the photographs of your drawings—he told me he knew your work, he had seen many, many of your drawings. They were in the archives of the armory in Baltimore, Maryland. I met him there a few months later.

We went into an old, musty conference room. I was in the process of writing this book and had conceived the format of each chapter consisting of one month, beginning with H-Hour, June, July, August, and on until the end of the war, May 1945. On the shelves of the archive were huge bound books. These were the After Action Reports of the 29th Division. Each volume was titled: H-Hour, June, July, August, etc. For each report of the 116th Regiment or the Military Police Platoon there was a cover drawing, H-Hour, June, July, August .... Astonishingly, they had been drawn by you!

I am, as you stated, "shakened." There was no way that I would have discovered these drawings, nor would anyone other than I know absolutely which drawings in the archives were done by you.

Sometimes I think that you were like one of those ancient Gods who came to earth to mate with a mortal. To make certain that the epic tale of war would be told truly.

As you lay dying you looked at your hands—to see the stigmata—yes, you were crucified—by that ghastly disease. Like Christ, you left disciples. For how else could this story be told? I'm the vessel through whom you wrote your book.

Here. Here is the book that "Giannini" wrote. I place it on your grave. Let me rest now, for I have loved you. "I love thee with the breath, smiles, tears, of all my life!—and if God choose, I shall but love thee better after death."

In 2003, we cleared the studio, completely. There, between two enormous boards of plywood, was your last work. Hidden. Four feet by five feet, an immense structure of crosses. Like Mozart's *Requiem Mass*, this last work is a final *Requiem, Omaha Beach, D-Day, June 6, 1944.*

# ACKNOWLEDGMENTS

I thought I was totally alone; first in discovering Ugo's letters and drawings and his last abstract war paintings. Then in researching and creating a book that could contain his work; that there was no one to thank. However, without a wonderful support system, this book would not have come into existence.

My profound thanks to David Lamb who said yes, he would publish the book. To Fiona Hallowell who was able to take the mass of material and streamline it into a coherent, lucid, elegantly written book. To Liz Driesbach, the art director who envisioned the space in which Ugo's prose and art could live.

My thank you to Micki Wesson who supported me emotionally and financially. To Simon Lipscar who believed in the genius of Ugo's work. To Joseph Balkoski who knew the historical importance of Ugo's writings and art. Thank you to Dr. William A. McIntosh for exhibiting Ugo's drawings at the first Monument called Overlord in Virginia. To Jeff Fulgham of the Overlord Monument who continued to exhibit Ugo's work. To the Maire of Vire, Jean Yves Cousin for his constant appreciation of Ugo's talent. Thank you Petra Chu for her brilliant writing about Ugo. To the many museums that have exhibited Ugo's war drawings. To Headquarters in Hamburg who exhibited Ugo's images for the 50th Anniversary of D-Day, June 6, 1994. To Howard and Joe Rehs of Rehs Galleries for exhibiting Ugo's works.

To my many friends who always said WOW when they viewed the book.

And lastly, my dear daughter Laura, and my son Mark who watched my struggle, and continued to believe it was worth it. And to Karen, and Antonio, the boy who calls me Meema.